ARCHITECTURA NAVALIS MERCATORIA,

NAVIUM varii generis *MERCATORIARUM, CAPULICARUM, CURSORIARUM, ALIARUMQUE,* cujuscunqve conditionis vel molis, Formas et rationes exhibens: exemplis æri incisis, Demonstrationibus denique. Dimensionibus calculisque accuratissimis illustrata.

Autore,

FRIDERICO HENR. CHAPMAN.

S.R. Majest: Naupego,
R. Acad. Scient: Svec: Membro.

HOLMIÆ Aᵒ MDCCLXVIII.

[Original title page]

ARCHITECTURA NAVALIS MERCATORIA

The Classic of Eighteenth-Century Naval Architecture

Fredrik Henrik af Chapman

DOVER PUBLICATIONS, INC.
Mineola, New York

Publisher's Note

Fredrik Henrik af Chapman (1721–1808), born in Sweden, was the first known naval architect to use scientific principles in his ship designs. As a young boy, Chapman would trail after his father, a captain at the Gothenburg Naval Dockyard, and draw ship body plans. One of these was so impressive that his father told a shipwright to produce the design in actual size. In 1738, Chapman became a shipbuilding apprentice in the same naval dockyard. He subsequently worked in various other dockyards, but grew dissatisfied with gaining practical experience by itself. Soon after, while working as a ship's carpenter in London, Chapman was able to study mathematics and physics so he could apply a more extensive knowledge to shipbuilding. With his advanced education, Chapman changed the fundamentals of ship construction—formerly a craft—into a meticulous science.

The present volume reproduces all sixty-two plates from Chapman's pioneering, eighteenth-century work entitled *Architectura Navalis Mercatoria*. First published in Stockholm in 1768, Chapman's carefully detailed work built his reputation as one of the greatest shipbuilders of all time. Following the plates is a republication of the James Inman translation of Chapman's *Tractat om Skepps-Byggeriet (A Treatise on Shipbuilding)*, which was completed several years after the plates appeared. Well over two centuries later, Chapman's work is kept alive through a continued interest in vessels of the past and the history of naval architecture. The magnificent line drawings that appear here document both merchant and naval ships from various countries. This exquisite collection of ships' plans and text, reprinted from one of the most treasured works of all time, will enthrall anyone fascinated by maritime architecture and design.

Bibliographical Note

This Dover edition, first published in 2006, contains sixty-two plates reprinted from *Architectura Navalis Mercatoria*, originally published by Holmiæ, Stockholm, in 1768. Following the plates is a republication of the James Inman translation of Chapman's *Tractat om Skepps-Byggeriet*, as originally published in *A Treatise on Shipbuilding, with explanations and demonstrations respecting the Architectura Navalis Mercatoria*, printed by J. Smith and sold by Deighton & Sons, Cambridge, in 1820.

Library of Congress Cataloging-in-Publication Data

Chapman, F. H. af (Fredrik Henrik), 1721–1808.
 Architectura navalis mercatoria : the classic of eighteenth-century naval architecture / Fredrik Henrik af Chapman.
  p. cm.
 Reprint. Stockholm : Holmiae, 1768.
  ISBN-13: 978-0-486-45155-8
  ISBN-10: 0-486-45155-0 (pbk.)
  1. Naval architecture. I. Title.

VM142.C523 2006
623.8'1—dc22

2006050211

Manufactured in the United States by Courier Corporation
45155004   2013
www.doverpublications.com

Contents

Index and descriptions of the draughts contained in this work   vi

The Plates   1

Author's Preface to the *Tractat om Skepps-Byggeriet,* 1775   125

On the resistance which a ship in motion meets from the water   128

On the dimensions of ships   133

On the proportions of privateers   138

On the proportions of masts and yards for merchant ships   145

On the construction of the scale of solidity   147

On the measurement for tonnage and stowage   149

On the accommodations for provisions   151

INDEX AND DESCRIPTION OF THE DRAUGHT

Merchant Ships or Veſſels.

Number of the Plate.	Number of the Draught.	Nature of the Veſſels, as to there Shape and Rigging.		Length between the pp:rs of Stem and Sternpoſt.	Breadth Moulded.	Draught of vather as it is on the Plan.	The greateſt Draught of wather, to which the Veſſel may reaſonably be loaded.	The real Burthen in Tons at the greateſt Draught of water.
		1:ſt Claſs.		Feet.	Feet.	Feet.	Feet.	
I.	1	Frigat built	Ships Rigging	160	$41\frac{5}{12}$	$22\frac{1}{12}$	$22\frac{1}{3}$	1140
II.	2	d:o	d:o	149	39	$20\frac{3}{4}$	$21\frac{1}{8}$	900
III.	3	d:o	d:o	136	36	19	$19\frac{1}{3}$	761
IV.	4	d:o	d:o	$124\frac{1}{6}$	$33\frac{2}{3}$	$17\frac{1}{2}$	$18\frac{1}{6}$	572
V.	5	d:o	d:o	115	$31\frac{1}{8}$	$16\frac{1}{12}$	$16\frac{2}{3}$	424
V.	6	d:o	d:o	$100\frac{1}{8}$	$28\frac{7}{12}$	$14\frac{1}{12}$	$14\frac{2}{3}$	307
VI.	7	d:o	d:o	89	26	13	$13\frac{3}{4}$	244
VI.	8	d:o	Snow Rigging	$77\frac{1}{3}$	23	$11\frac{1}{3}$	$11\frac{11}{12}$	159
VII.	9	d:o	Scooner Rigging	$79\frac{1}{2}$	$20\frac{7}{12}$	$8\frac{1}{12}$	$8\frac{7}{12}$	115
VII.	10	d:o	Sloop Rigging	$54\frac{1}{4}$	18	$8\frac{1}{3}$	$8\frac{1}{4}$	65
		2:d Claſs.						
VIII.	11	Hagboat	d:o	$156\frac{1}{8}$	$38\frac{11}{12}$	$21\frac{1}{3}$	$21\frac{1}{8}$	1164
IX.	12	d:o	d:o	$144\frac{1}{4}$	$36\frac{5}{8}$	$19\frac{5}{8}$	$19\frac{5}{8}$	903
X.	13	d:o	d:o	$132\frac{1}{2}$	$34\frac{1}{3}$	$18\frac{3}{4}$	$18\frac{1}{2}$	716
XI.	14	d:o	d:o	$122\frac{5}{12}$	$32\frac{1}{8}$	$16\frac{5}{8}$	$17\frac{1}{12}$	548
		3:d Claſs.						
XII.	15	Pink	Ships Rigging	$109\frac{5}{8}$	$29\frac{1}{4}$	$15\frac{1}{3}$	$15\frac{1}{3}$	416
XII.	16	d:o	d:to	$97\frac{1}{4}$	$26\frac{1}{4}$	$13\frac{11}{12}$	$14\frac{1}{3}$	309
XIII.	17	d:o	Snow Rigging	86	$24\frac{5}{12}$	$12\frac{5}{12}$	$12\frac{5}{8}$	215
XIII.	18	d:o	Briggantine Rigging	$74\frac{1}{2}$	$21\frac{2}{3}$	$10\frac{1}{4}$	$11\frac{7}{12}$	149
XIV.	19	d:o	d:o	$62\frac{5}{8}$	$18\frac{1}{4}$	$9\frac{1}{4}$	$9\frac{2}{3}$	89
XIV.	20	d:o	Sloop Rigging	$51\frac{1}{4}$	$16\frac{7}{12}$	$7\frac{1}{4}$	$8\frac{1}{8}$	52
		4:th Claſs.						
XV.	21	Catt	Ships Rigging	$151\frac{3}{4}$	$37\frac{1}{2}$	$19\frac{1}{2}$	$19\frac{1}{2}$	1097
XVI.	22	d:o	d:o	141	$35\frac{1}{2}$	$18\frac{1}{2}$	$18\frac{1}{2}$	833
XVII.	23	d:o	d:o	$130\frac{1}{4}$	$33\frac{1}{12}$	$17\frac{1}{2}$	$17\frac{1}{2}$	711
XVIII.	24	d:o	d:o	$118\frac{1}{3}$	$30\frac{1}{2}$	$16\frac{1}{12}$	$16\frac{7}{12}$	575
XVIII.	25	d:o	d:o	$106\frac{1}{2}$	28	$14\frac{11}{12}$	$15\frac{1}{2}$	446
XIX.	26	d:o	d:o	$95\frac{5}{12}$	$25\frac{7}{12}$	$13\frac{1}{3}$	$13\frac{5}{8}$	340
XIX.	27	d:o	Snow Rigging	$83\frac{1}{2}$	$22\frac{5}{8}$	$11\frac{11}{12}$	$12\frac{1}{2}$	237
XX.	28	d:o	Briggantine Rigging	72	$20\frac{1}{4}$	$10\frac{1}{4}$	$10\frac{11}{12}$	153
XX.	29	d:o	Sloop Rigging	$60\frac{1}{4}$	18	$8\frac{1}{4}$	$9\frac{5}{12}$	93
XX.	30	d:o	d:to	$48\frac{1}{2}$	$15\frac{5}{12}$	$7\frac{1}{8}$	$7\frac{1}{8}$	43
		5:te Claſs.						
XXI.	31	Bark	Ships Rigging	$150\frac{1}{4}$	38	20	$20\frac{5}{8}$	1257
XXII.	32	d:o	d:o	$138\frac{5}{12}$	$33\frac{1}{4}$	$18\frac{1}{2}$	$19\frac{1}{2}$	996
XXIII.	33	d:o	d:o	$127\frac{1}{4}$	$32\frac{1}{4}$	$17\frac{1}{3}$	$18\frac{5}{8}$	840
XXIV.	34	d:o	d:to	$115\frac{2}{3}$	$29\frac{10}{12}$	$15\frac{1}{4}$	$16\frac{1}{2}$	608
XXIV.	35	d:o	d:o	$103\frac{5}{8}$	27	$14\frac{1}{4}$	15	455
XXV.	36	d:o	Snow Rigging	$92\frac{1}{4}$	$24\frac{1}{4}$	$12\frac{5}{6}$	$13\frac{1}{3}$	316
XXV.	37	d:o	Briggantine Rigging	$80\frac{1}{4}$	$21\frac{2}{3}$	$11\frac{1}{4}$	$11\frac{5}{8}$	227
XXVI.	38	d:o	d:to	$68\frac{5}{8}$	$19\frac{1}{2}$	$9\frac{1}{2}$	$10\frac{1}{4}$	139
XXVI.	39	d:o	Sloop d:o	$57\frac{1}{3}$	$17\frac{2}{3}$	$8\frac{1}{4}$	$8\frac{7}{12}$	84
XXVI.	40	d:o	d:o	$45\frac{1}{4}$	15	$6\frac{2}{3}$	$6\frac{5}{8}$	41
		Veſſels of ſmall Draught of Water.						
XXVII.	1	Flyboat	Ships Rigging	$128\frac{1}{4}$	$29\frac{7}{12}$	$11\frac{1}{4}$	$14\frac{1}{12}$	618
XXVIII.	2	Bark	d:o	$108\frac{2}{3}$	$26\frac{1}{3}$	$9\frac{3}{4}$	$12\frac{5}{12}$	416
XXVIII.	3	d:o	Snow Rigging	$93\frac{1}{4}$	$23\frac{5}{12}$	$8\frac{3}{4}$	$10\frac{11}{12}$	258
XXVII.	4	d:o	Scooner Rigging	80	$21\frac{1}{2}$	8	9	159
XIV.	5	d:o	Galleas Rigging	68	$19\frac{1}{2}$	$7\frac{5}{8}$	$8\frac{1}{4}$	110
VII.	6	d:o	Sloop	$58\frac{1}{2}$	$17\frac{7}{12}$	$7\frac{7}{12}$	$7\frac{11}{12}$	84
XXIX.	7	d:o	Briggantine	$72\frac{5}{12}$	$20\frac{1}{3}$	$8\frac{1}{3}$	$9\frac{1}{8}$	142
XXIX.	8	d:o	Kray Rigging	72	$18\frac{1}{2}$	$6\frac{7}{12}$	$6\frac{1}{4}$	81
XXIX.	9	d:o	Sloop	45	$14\frac{2}{3}$	$5\frac{5}{12}$	$5\frac{5}{12}$	30
XXIX.	10	d:o	d:o	$37\frac{1}{8}$	$13\frac{2}{3}$	$4\frac{2}{3}$	$4\frac{2}{3}$	17
XXX.	11	Pink	Ketch Rigging	$78\frac{1}{4}$	$25\frac{7}{12}$	$10\frac{1}{4}$	$10\frac{1}{4}$	137
XXX.	12	Hoy	Chalke	67	$17\frac{2}{3}$	$6\frac{5}{8}$	$7\frac{7}{12}$	110
XXX.	13	Bark	Galleas	67	$21\frac{3}{8}$	$7\frac{5}{8}$	$7\frac{5}{8}$	93
XXVIII.	14	d:o	d:o	$62\frac{1}{2}$	$16\frac{1}{4}$	$6\frac{1}{3}$	$6\frac{5}{8}$	74
XXX.	15	Lighter		$49\frac{1}{3}$	$13\frac{3}{4}$ à $15\frac{3}{4}$	$5\frac{5}{12}$	$5\frac{5}{12}$	41
XXX.	16	Ferry boat		$49\frac{1}{2}$	$11\frac{1}{4}$	2	- -	- -

Veſſels for Swift Sailing and Rowin

Number of the Plate.	Number of the Draught.	What kind of Veſſels.	Length between the perpend. of Stem and Stern Poſt.	Breadth Moulded.	Draught of wather.	
		Packet Boats.	Feet.	Feet.	Feet.	
XLI.	1	Frigat	$81\frac{2}{3}$	$22\frac{7}{12}$	$10\frac{2}{3}$	-
XLI.	2	Scooner	$73\frac{5}{8}$	$18\frac{1}{2}$	$8\frac{2}{3}$	-
XLII.	3	Sloop, with two ſorts of Frames, for more or leſs draught of water	$60\frac{5}{12}$	$17\frac{7}{12}$	$\{8\frac{1}{8}$ / $5\frac{11}{12}$	-
XLII.	4	Scooner	$54\frac{7}{12}$	$15\frac{7}{12}$	$7\frac{1}{12}$	-
XLII.	5	Sloop or Yacht	$38\frac{1}{4}$	$13\frac{1}{4}$	$5\frac{1}{2}$	-
		Pleaſure Veſſels. For Sailing.				
XLIII.	1	Frigat	$76\frac{1}{3}$	$22\frac{5}{12}$	$8\frac{1}{3}$	-
XLIII.	2	Scooner	$71\frac{11}{12}$	$18\frac{7}{12}$	$6\frac{11}{12}$	6
XLIV.	3	Yacht	$52\frac{5}{12}$	$17\frac{1}{12}$	$6\frac{1}{3}$	-
XLIV.	4	Scooner	$62\frac{3}{8}$	$16\frac{1}{3}$	$5\frac{5}{8}$	6
XLV.	5	Yacht	$42\frac{1}{4}$	$14\frac{5}{8}$	5	-
XLV.	6	Yacht	35	13	$4\frac{5}{12}$	-
XLIV.	7	Yacht	$31\frac{1}{3}$	$10\frac{1}{2}$	$3\frac{1}{12}$	-
XLV.	8	Yacht	$29\frac{1}{3}$	$11\frac{1}{4}$	4	-
XLV.	9	Yacht	$25\frac{1}{3}$	$10\frac{1}{8}$	$3\frac{1}{2}$	-
XLIV.	10	Yacht	$23\frac{5}{12}$	$7\frac{7}{12}$	$2\frac{1}{3}$	-
		Pleaſure Veſſels. For Rowing.				
XLVI.	1	a Row Galley	$121\frac{1}{8}$	$18\frac{1}{2}$	$6\frac{5}{8}$	16
XLVI.	2	a Barge	$56\frac{7}{12}$	$10\frac{7}{12}$	$2\frac{7}{12}$	10
XLVII.	3	Barge	$50\frac{5}{12}$	$7\frac{1}{4}$	2	
XLVII.	4	Barge	$42\frac{1}{4}$	$6\frac{5}{12}$	2	
XLVII.	5	Barge	$35\frac{1}{4}$	$6\frac{1}{12}$	$1\frac{2}{3}$	
XLVII.	6	Pinnace	$27\frac{1}{4}$	$5\frac{5}{8}$	$1\frac{2}{3}$	7
XLVII.	7	Pinnace	$23\frac{5}{12}$	$5\frac{5}{12}$	$1\frac{2}{3}$	
XLVII.	8	Pinnace or yawle	$19\frac{1}{4}$	$4\frac{5}{8}$	$1\frac{1}{4}$	
		Boats, Large and Small for the uſe of Ships.				
XIV.	1	Launce	$36\frac{1}{2}$	$9\frac{5}{8}$	- -	8
XLVIII.	2	Launce	$29\frac{1}{3}$	$8\frac{1}{2}$	- -	7
XLVIII.	3	Launce	$24\frac{5}{12}$	$7\frac{1}{8}$	- -	
XXVI.	4	Launce	$19\frac{5}{12}$	$5\frac{5}{8}$	- -	
XLVIII.	5	Longboat	$33\frac{1}{3}$	$9\frac{1}{4}$	- -	8
XLVIII.	6	Longboat	$29\frac{1}{4}$	9	- -	7
XLVIII.	7	Longboat	$25\frac{1}{3}$	$8\frac{1}{12}$	- -	
XLVIII.	8	Longboat	$21\frac{1}{2}$	$7\frac{5}{12}$	- -	
XLVIII.	9	Longboat or yawle	$17\frac{7}{12}$	$6\frac{1}{2}$	- -	
XXVI.	1	Barge or Pinnace	$32\frac{1}{6}$	$6\frac{1}{4}$	- -	
VII.	2	Pinnace	$29\frac{1}{3}$	$6\frac{1}{12}$	- -	
XIII.	3	Pinnace	$26\frac{1}{4}$	$5\frac{11}{12}$	- -	
XIII.	4	Pinnace	$23\frac{1}{4}$	$5\frac{5}{8}$	- -	
XX.	5	Yawle	$19\frac{1}{2}$	$5\frac{5}{6}$	- -	
XX.	6	Yawle	$17\frac{7}{12}$	$5\frac{2}{3}$	- -	
XXV.	7	Yawle	$15\frac{5}{12}$	$5\frac{1}{3}$	- -	
XXV.	8	Yawle	$13\frac{7}{12}$	$5\frac{7}{12}$	- -	
XXV.	9	Yawle	$11\frac{7}{12}$	$4\frac{5}{8}$	- -	
XLVIII.	10	Yawle	$9\frac{1}{4}$	$4\frac{1}{4}$	- -	
XLVIII.	11	Perogue	$18\frac{1}{4}$	$4\frac{1}{8}$	- -	2
LIII.	10	Boat for Sailing on the Ice	- -	- -	- -	
	11	Proportion of Sails for the ſame	- -	- -	- -	

STOCKHOLM, Printed by JOHN GEORGE LANGE, r

CONTAINED IN THIS WORK.

Privateers.

Plate	Number of the Draught.	Nature of the Vessels, as to there Rigging.	Total Number of Carriage Guns.	Number of Guns and Weight of the Ball. On Deck. Number	On Deck. P:d Shot	On Quarter-deck and Fore-Castle. Number	On Quarter-deck and Fore-Castle. P:d Shot	Swivel Guns. Number	Swivel Guns. P:d Shot	Length between the perp:rs of Stem and Sternpost.	Breadth Moulded.	Draught of Water abaft.	Height of Gunports above Water a Midships.	Number of Men including Officers.	Months Provision.	Months Water.	Pair of Oars.
										Feet.	Feet.	Feet.	Feet.				
XI.	1	Frigat	40	28	18	12	6	---	---	156 1/7	39¼	18	8¼	400	5	2½	---
III.	2	Frigat	38	26	18	12	6	---	---	145½	38	17	6¾	360	5	2½	---
.IV.	3	Frigat	34	24	12	10	4	---	---	135	34½	15½	6¾	310	4½	2¼	---
XV.	4	Frigat	32	24	9	8	3	---	--	125	32½	14½	5½	260	4¼	2⅛	7
VI.	5	Frigat	22	20	6	2	4	32	3	116½	30½	14¼	4¼	220	4	2	7
VII.	6	Frigat	18	18	6	---	---	22	3	109	29¼	12 9/10	4¼	200	4	2	12
III.	7	Frigat	16	16	6	---	---	---	---	100¼	26¼	11½	4¼	160	3	1½	11
III.	8	Snow	14	14	4	---	---	12	3	90½	24½	10¼	4½	115	3	1½	10
IX.	9	Ketch	12	12	4	---	---	---	---	83	22¾	9¾	3 9/10	90	2½	1¼	9
IX.	10	Ketch	11	10	3	1	18	---	---	74	20½	8½	3 9/10	70	2	1	8
XL.	11	Scooner	2	---	---	2	6	32	3	93½	23⅛	9¼	----	100	2	1	10
XL.	12	Scooner	2	2	4	---	---	10	3	70	18½	7⅛	----	50	2	1	8
XL.	13	Sloop	10	8	3	2	6	---	---	62¼	20½	7¼	3¼	50	2	1	7
.II.		Sections and Contrivances of the Privateer N:o 1.															

Several kinds of Vessels used by different Nations.

Number of the Draught.	Kind of Vessels.	Length between the perp. of Stem and Stern Post.	Bredth Moulded.	Draught of Water.	Total number of Carriage Guns.	Number of Guns and weight of ball. On Deck. Numb.	On Deck. P. Shot.	Quardeck and Forecastle. Numb.	Quardeck and Forecastle. P. Shot.	Swivel Guns.	Musquetoons.	Pair of Oars.
	Vessels of War.	Feet.	Feet.	Feet.			p.		p.			
9	La Sirenne, a French Frigat	127¼	33½	15⅜	34	26	9	8	4	-	-	-
10	The Unicorn, an Engelish Frigat	122½	33 5/12	17	34	24	9	10	4	-	-	-
11	Jaramas, a Swedish Frigat	122¼	32	16¾	32	22	9	10	4	-	-	-
12	Blau Hagern, a Danish Frigat	86½	22¾	11¼	18	18	4	- -	- -	-	-	-
14	Neptunus, a Privateer, Built at Ostende	79¾	22¾	11½	16	16	6	- -	- -	8	-	9
15	a Bermuda Sloop	60¼	21⅝	12¼	10	10	4	- -	- -	12	-	-
16	a French Tartane	61	17⅜	6½	8	8	4	- -	- -	4	-	-
17	an Algerine Chebec	127	25½	9½	28	16	6	4 / 8	12 / 3	-	30	9
18	La Capitana, a Row Gally of Malta	179½	24¼	8½	5	2 / 2	[illegible]	1	36	18	18	30
1	The Carolina Yacht, belonging to his Brittanik Majesty	90¾	24	10	8	8	4	- -	- -	6	-	-
6	an English Cutter	54	22 5/12	10¼	12	12	3	- -	- -	14	-	5
	Merchant Ships or Vessels.											
1	an English East Indiaman	129¼	33½	19¾						-	-	-
2	an English WestIndia Trader	97	27	15¼						-	-	-
3	a French Trader, River Built	57½	17¼	10	- -	- -	- -	- -	- -	-	-	-
5	Le Chameau Flute, a French Store Ship	147½	31⅔	14⅝	- -	- -	- -	- -	- -	-	-	-
6	a Dutch Flyboat	132½	29¾	14½	- -	- -	- -	- -	- -	-	-	-
7	a Dutch Smack	87⅞	22	8	- -	- -	- -	- -	- -	-	-	-
8	a Dutch Hoy, with Three Masts	107⅞	26¾	13¼	- -	- -	- -	- -	- -	-	-	-
7	a Dutch Hoy with two masts	81	23	9⅛	- -	- -	- -	- -	- -	-	-	-
9	a Scoote, used by the Finlanders	61½	25	7⅝	- -	- -	- -	- -	- -	-	-	-

Number of the Plate.	Number of the Draught.	Kind of Vessels.	Length between the perp. of Stem and Sternpost.	Breadth Moulded.	Draught of water.
		Fishing Vessels.	Feet.	Feet.	feet
LIX.	1	a Dutch Dogger, for Carrying Lobsters	63	18⅔	8¾
LIX.	2	an English Herring Buss	66	16⅝	9
LIX.	3	an English Smack for Flattfish	58½	13¼	6 5/12
LX.	4	a Vessel with a well for Carrying Fish used at Stockholm	42⅔	12⅝	-
LX.	5	One d:o less of the same Kind.	17⅔	5⅝	-
		Different sorts of smaller Vessels.			
LVI.	19	Galleass, a Baltick Vessel	48½	14 5/12	5⅜
L.	7	a Spannish Bark, used in Cadix	44	12½	-
L.	11	an English Hoy or Lighther	51	16½	8
L.	12	a Hopper, for Carrying of Ballast	37¼	16⅓	-
L.	13	Chalk Barge, an English Vessel	56	15½	-
LII.	4	a Close Lighter, English	42½	18 5/12	5⅝
XLIX.	2	an 8 oared Barge, English	43⅝	6⅝	-
XLIX.	3	a Dutch Heeren Yacht	46¾	15 7/12	-
XLIX.	4	a Dutch Scout or Boyert	25½	8½	-
L.	5	a Swedish Boyert, or Pleasure boat	34⅞	11½	
L.	6	a Norway Yawl for Sailing	20¾	7¾	-
L.	8	a Venetian Gondole	36⅝	4½	-
L.	9	a English Wherry	26	5	-
L.	10	a Greenland Pinnace, for Whale fishery	24½	5¼	-
XLI.	14	a French Pinnace of 6 oars	30½	7½	-
LX.	8	a French Felouque of 10 pair of oars.	42½	8 7/12	-

Launching and manner of Rigging.

XI. Three different Methods of Launching Ships N:o 1. The French, N:o 2. the English, and N:o 3. The Dutch.

XII. Several Figures, Representing the different manners of Rigging, which are most in use in the Northern Contrys.

Frigat or Ship.	N:o 7. Dogger.	N:o 13. a Dutch Chalke.	N:o 19. a Longboat.
Snow.	N:o 8. Dutch Hoy.	N:o 14. English Hoy.	N:o 20. Deal Cutter.
Ketch.	N:o 9. Galleass, used in the Baltick.	N:o 15. English Cutter.	N:o 21. Pinnace.
Brigg.	N:o 10. Kray, used in Finland.	N:o 16. Tartane, with Latin Sails.	N:o 22. French Fishingboat, on the Coast of Britany
Billander.	N:o 11. Ketch-yacht, used in the Baltick.	N:o 17. Pleasure boat or Yacht.	N:o 23. Yawle.
Scooner.	N:o 12. Sloop.	N:o 18. French Longboat, with a Latin Sail.	N:o 24. Yawle, used by the Pilots at Stockholm.

Pl. I.

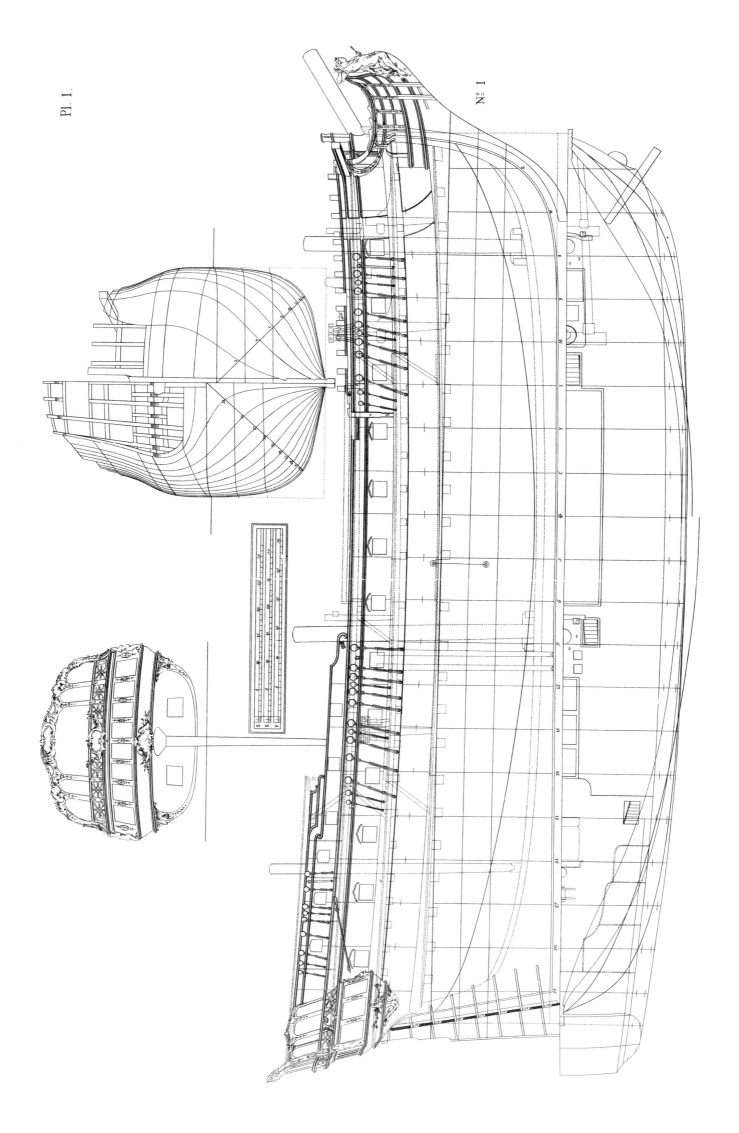

Pl. II

N.º 2

Pl. III.

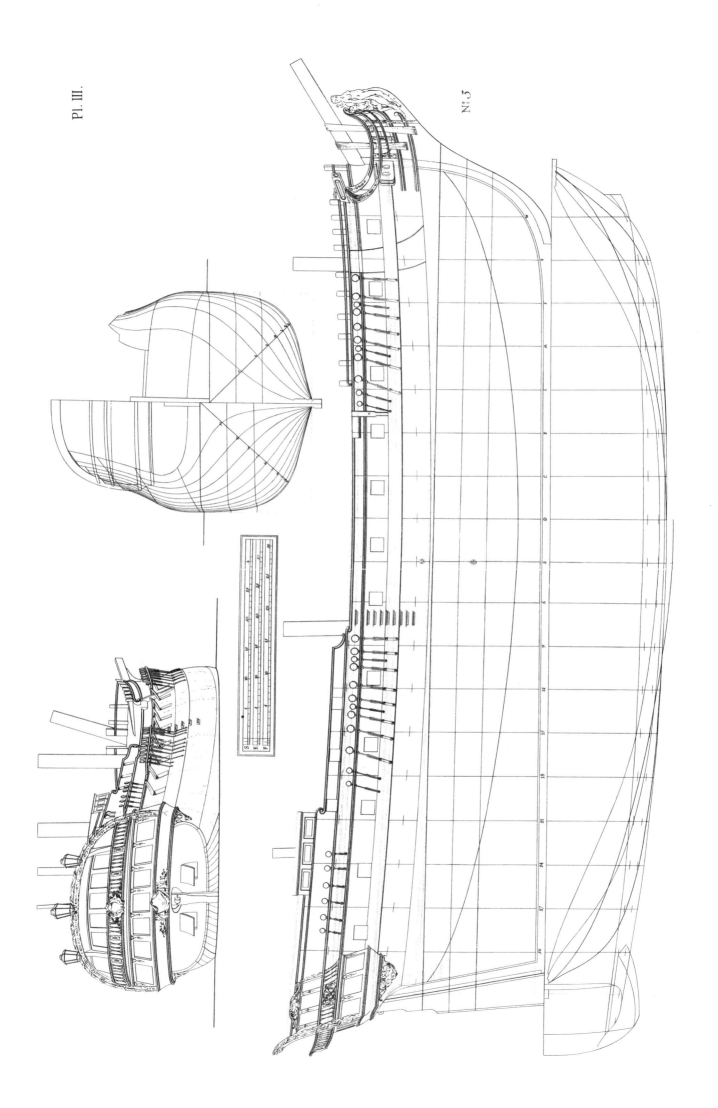

Pl. IV.

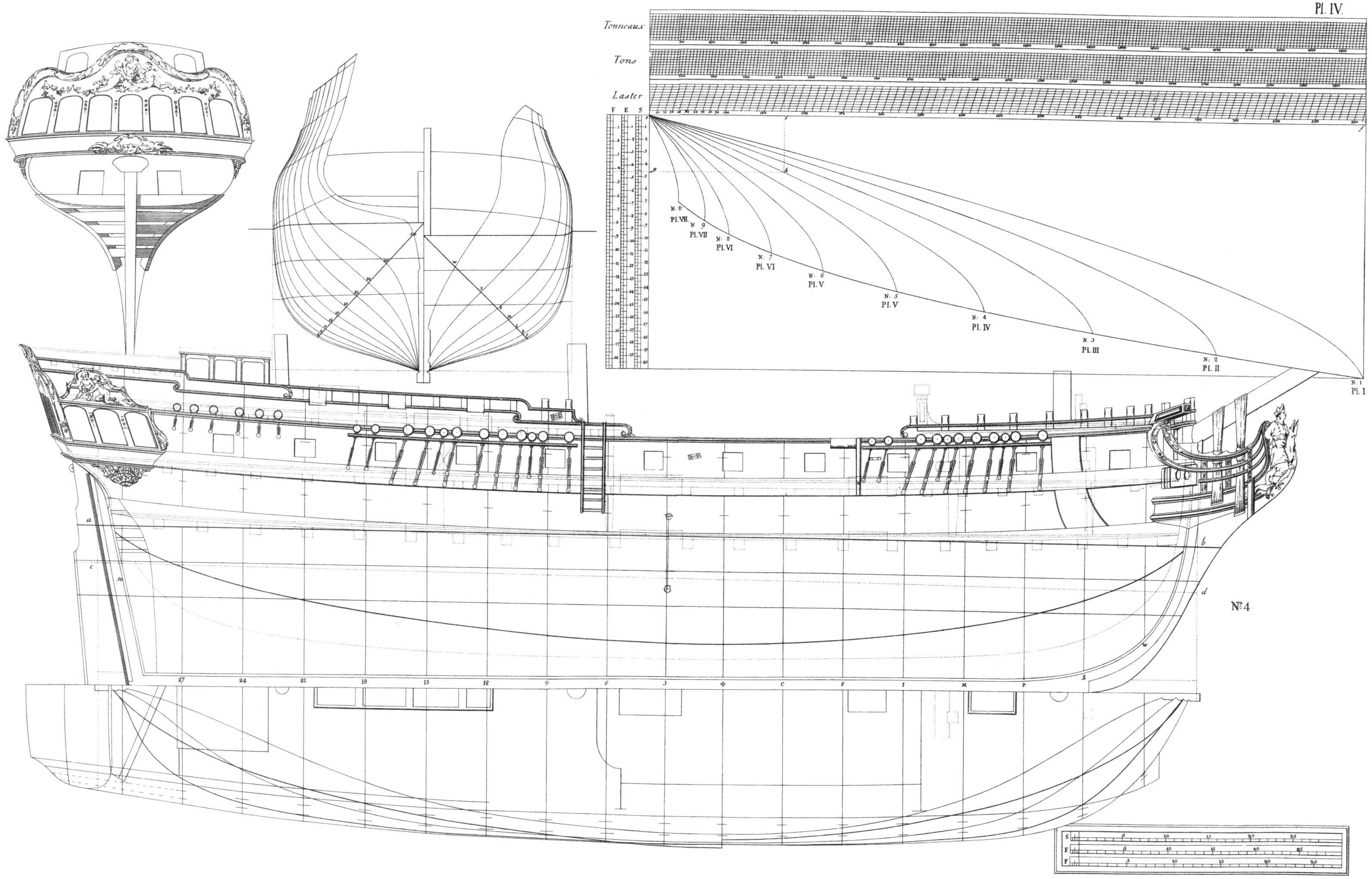

N.º 1
Pl. I

N.º 2
Pl. II

N.º 3
Pl. III

N.º 4
Pl. IV

N.º 5
Pl. V

N.º 6
Pl. V

N.º 7
Pl. VI

N.º 8
Pl. VI

N.º 9
Pl. VII

N.º O
Pl. VII

Tonneaux

Tons

Laster

F E S

N.º 4

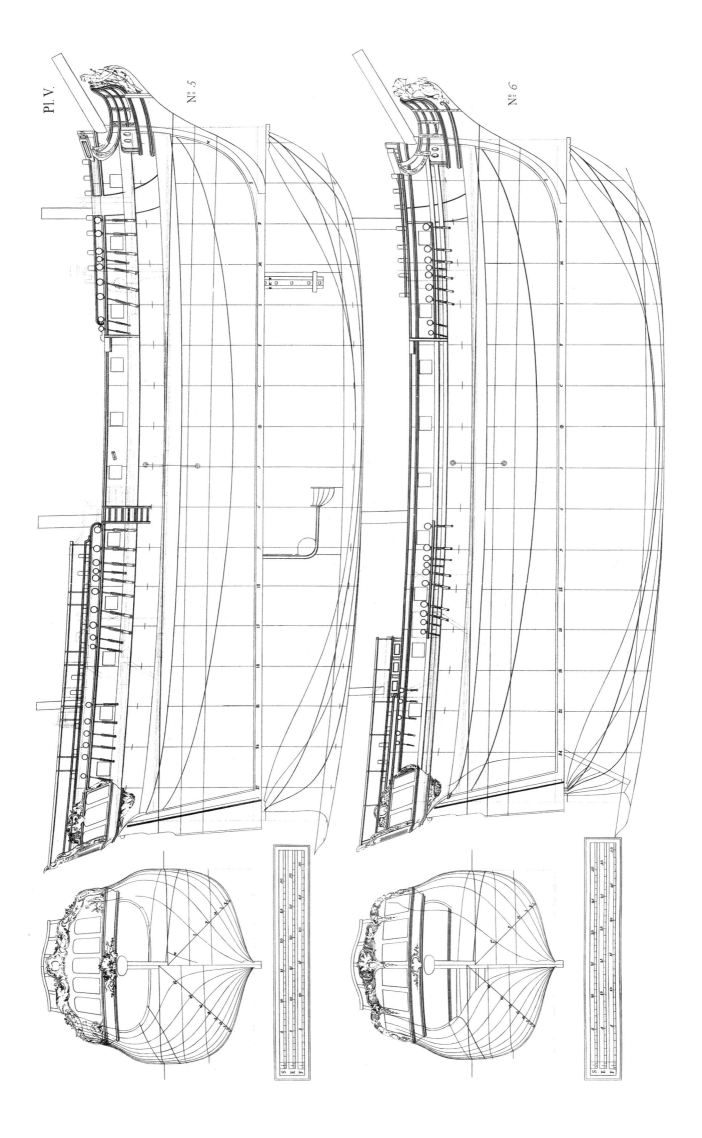

Pl. V.

N.º 5

N.º 6

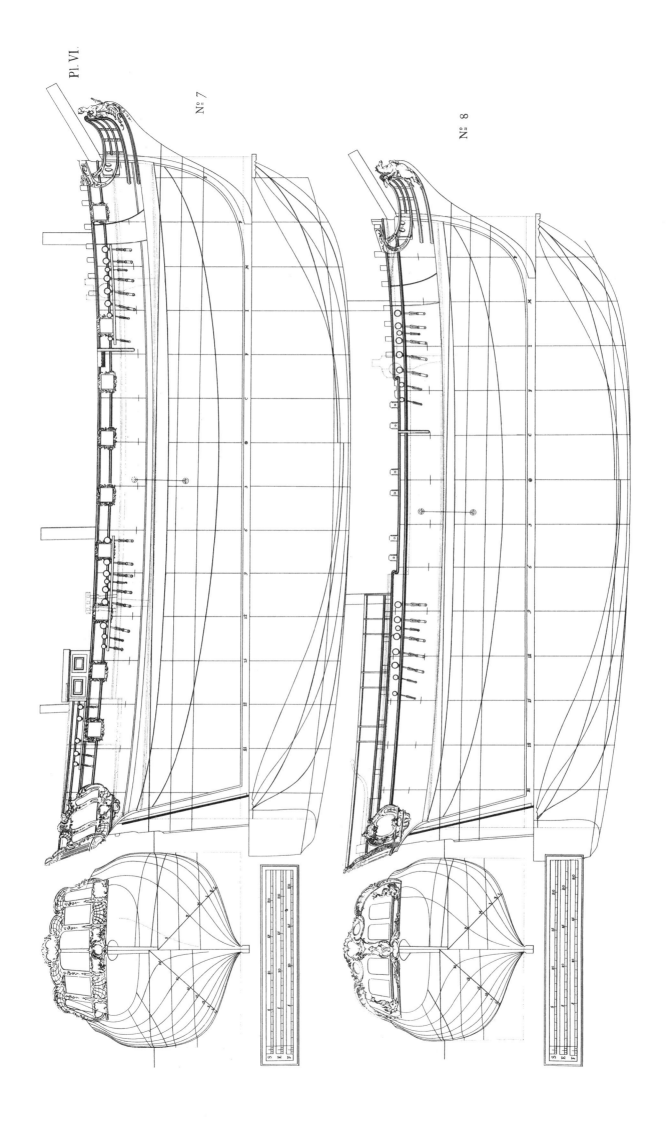

Pl. VI.

Nᵒ 7

Nᵒ 8

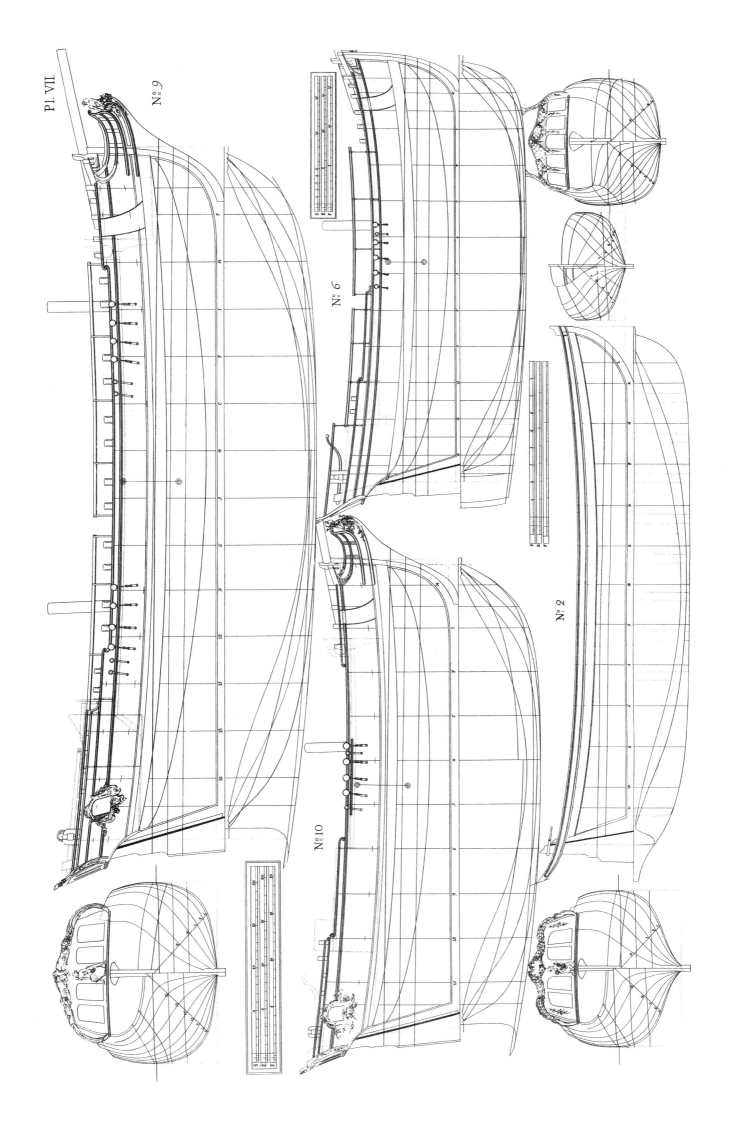

Pl. VII.

Nᵒ 9

Nᵒ 6

Nᵒ 2

Nᵒ 10

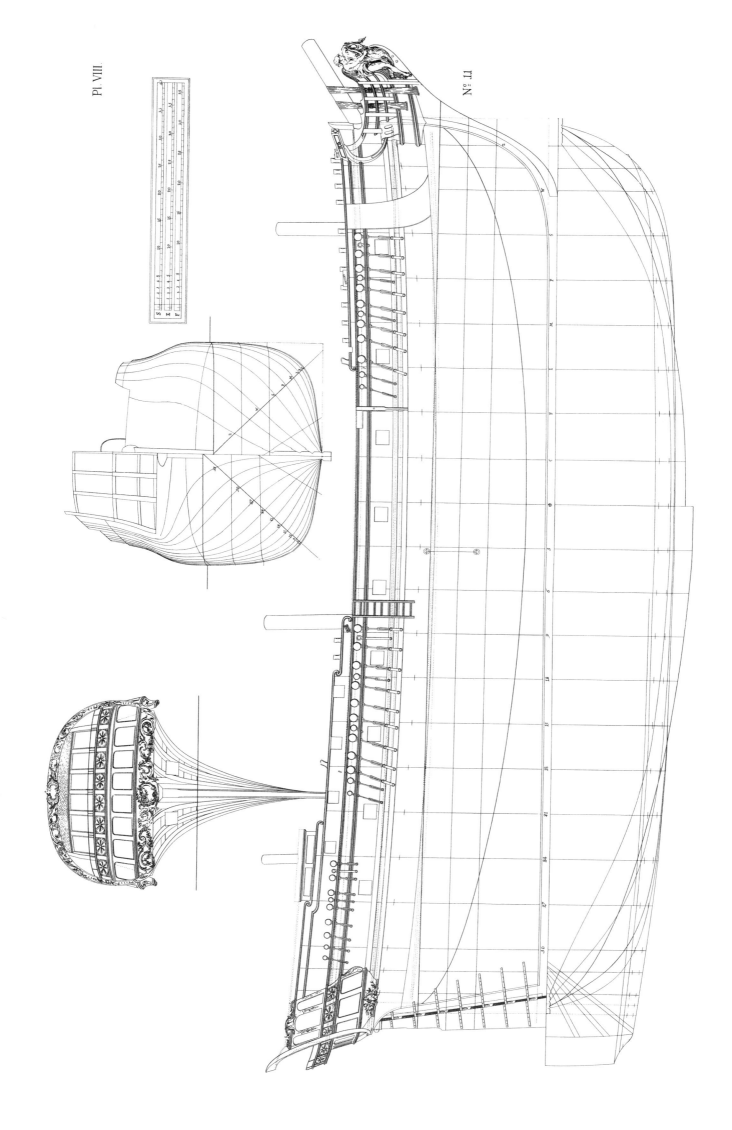

N.º II.

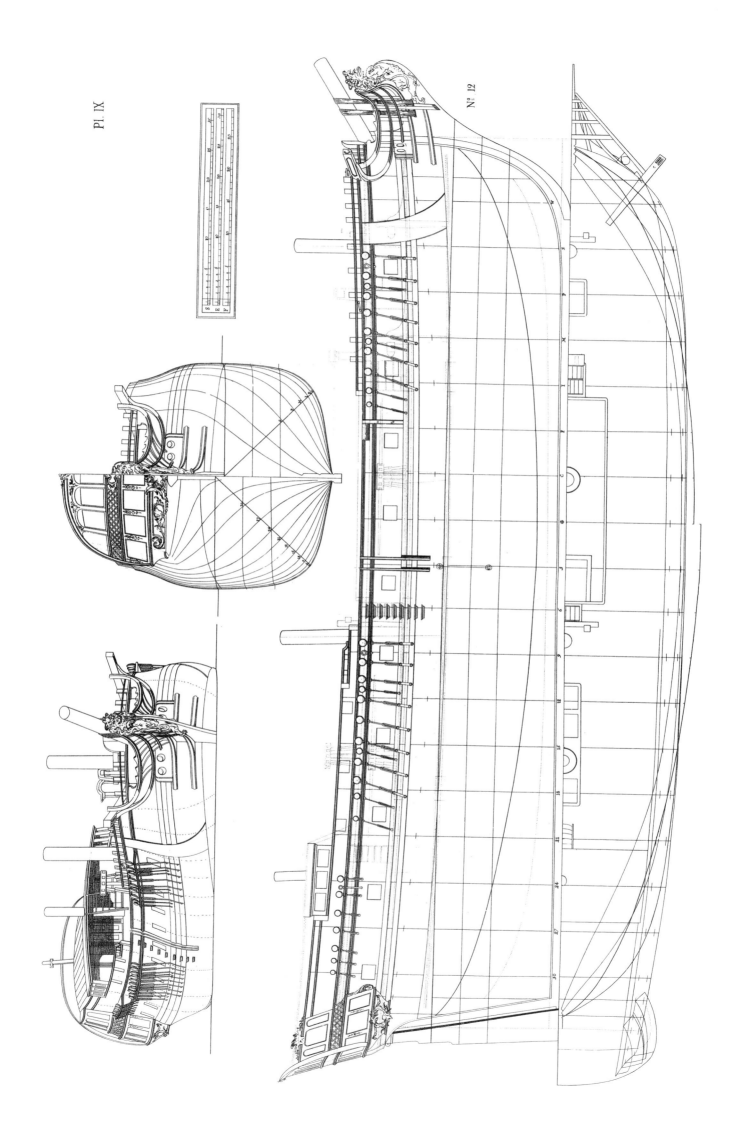

Pl. IX

Nº 12

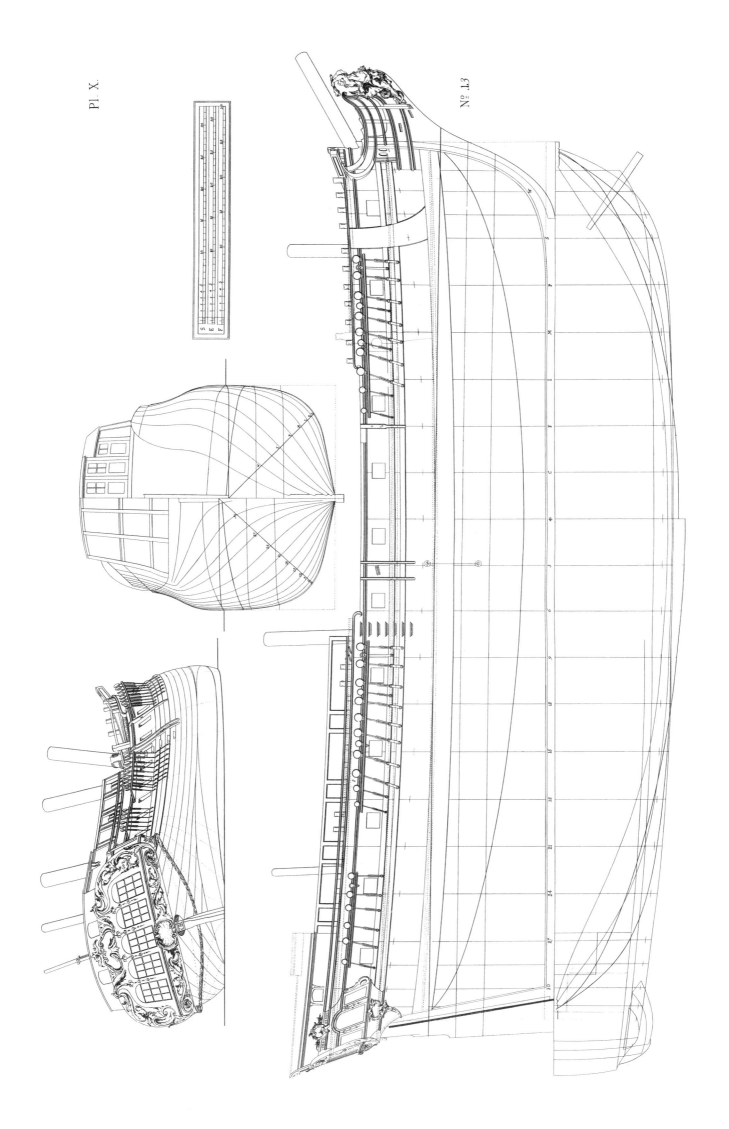

Pl. X.

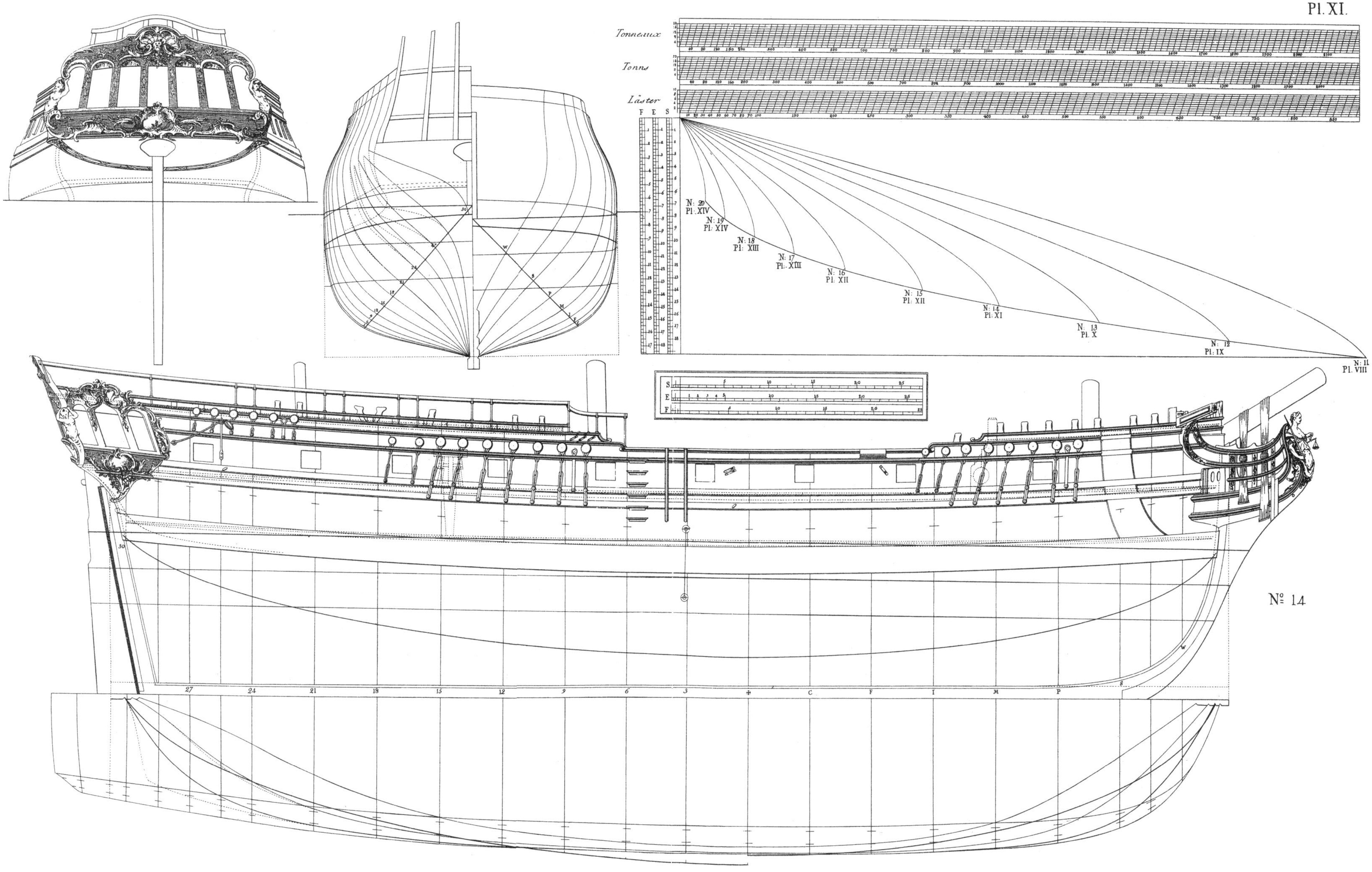

Pl. XI.

N° 14

N. 11
Pl. VIII

N. 12
Pl. IX

N. 13
Pl. X

N. 14
Pl. XI

N. 15
Pl. XII

N. 16
Pl. XIII

N. 17
Pl. XIII

N. 18
Pl. XIII

N. 19
Pl. XIV

N. 20
Pl. XIV

Tonneaux

Tonnu

Lister

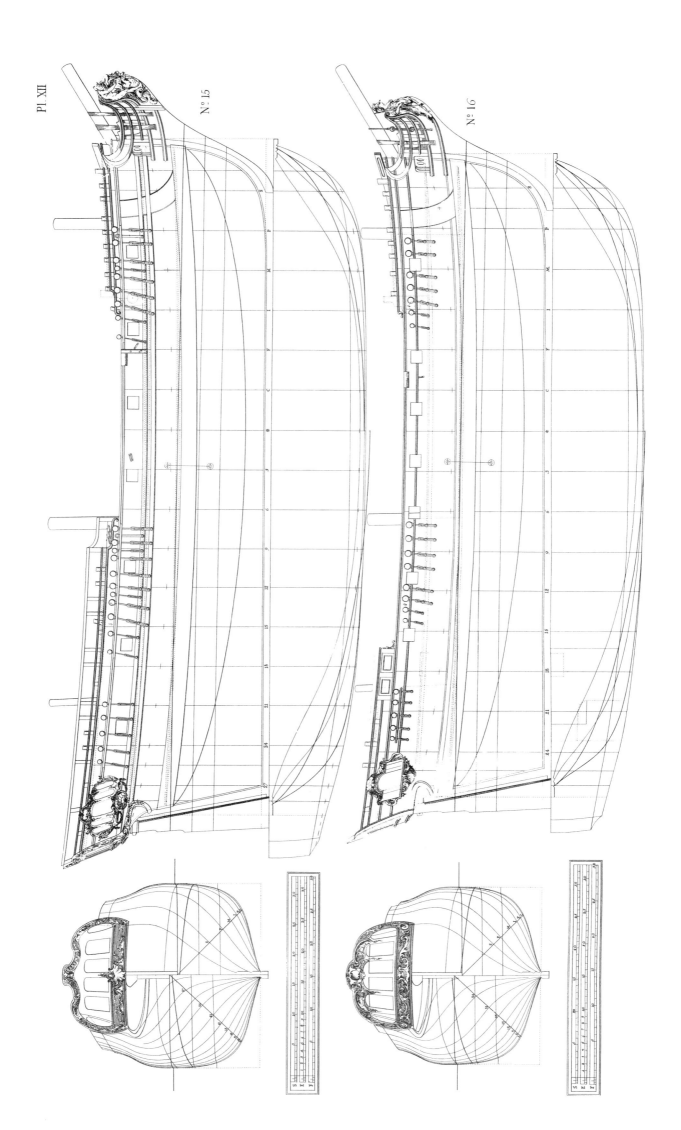

Pl. XII

Nº 15

Nº 16

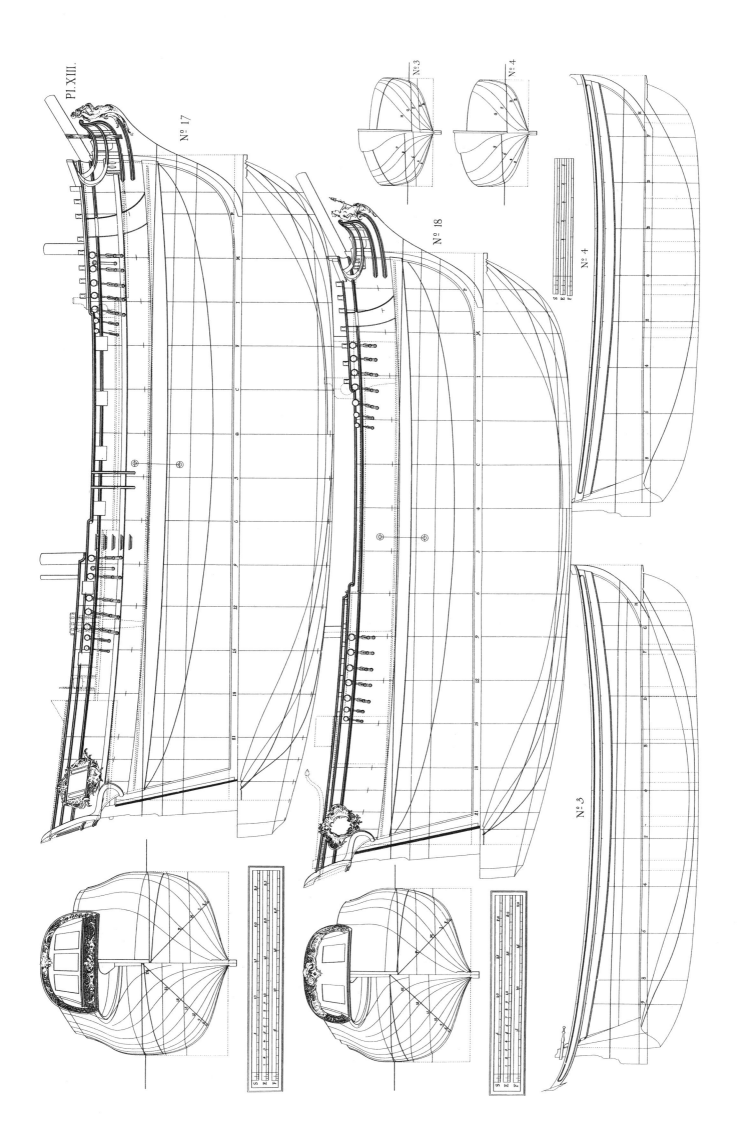

Pl. XIII.

N.° 17

N.° 18

N.° 3

N.° 4

N.° 3

N.° 4

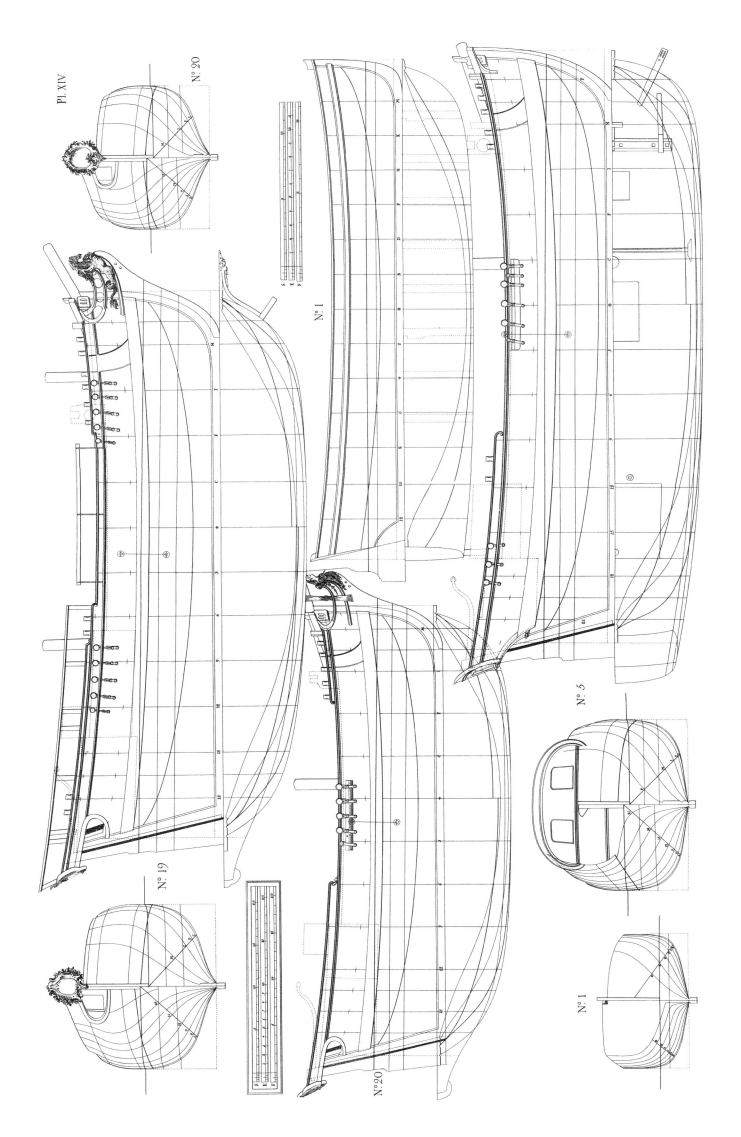

Pl. XIV.

N.º 20

N.º 1

N.º 19

N.º 20

N.º 5

N.º 1

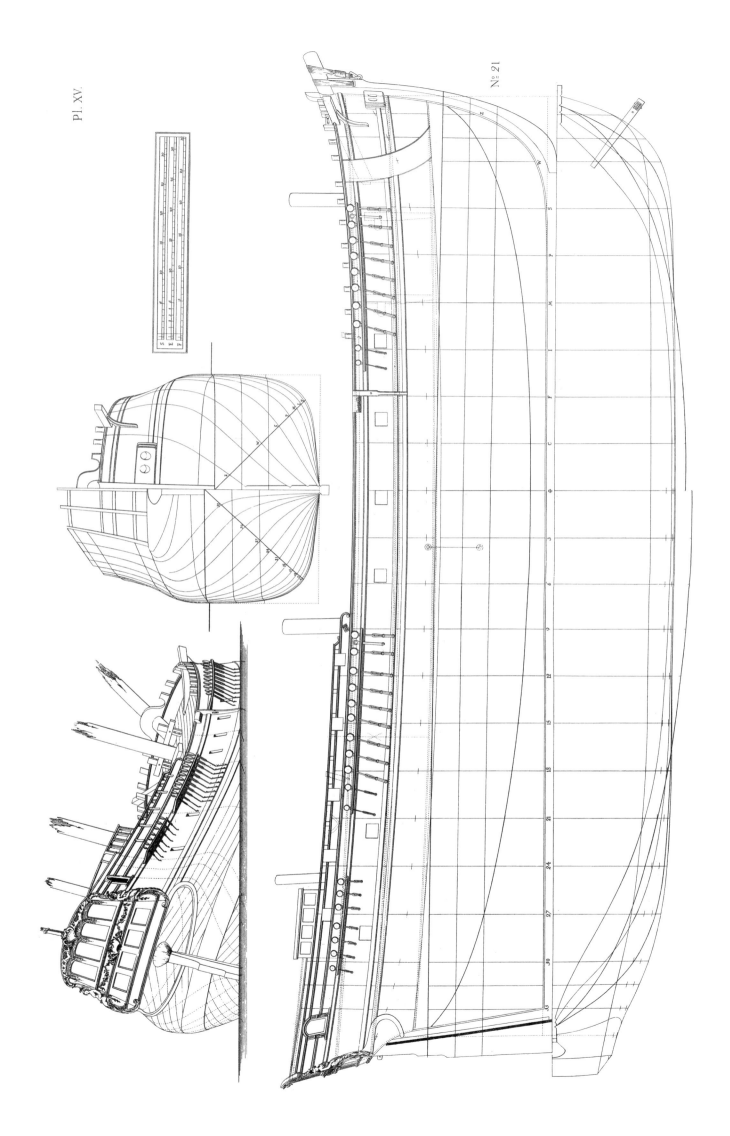

Pl. XV.

N.º 21

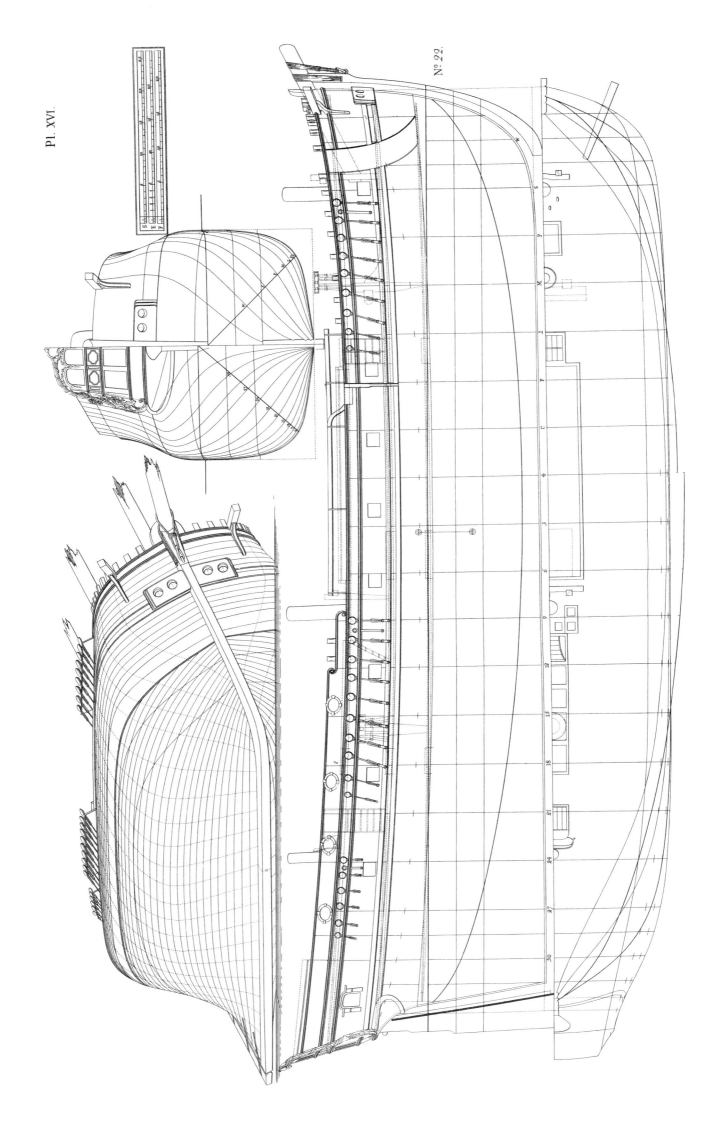

Pl. XVI.

Nº 22.

Pl. XVII.

Nº 23

N. 21
Pl. XV

N. 22
Pl. XVI

N. 23
Pl. XVII

N. 24
Pl. XVIII

N. 25
Pl. XVIII

N. 26
Pl. XIX

N. 27
Pl. XIX

N. 28
Pl. XX

N. 29
Pl. XX

N. 30
Pl. XX

Tonneaux

Tonnes

Lester

F E S

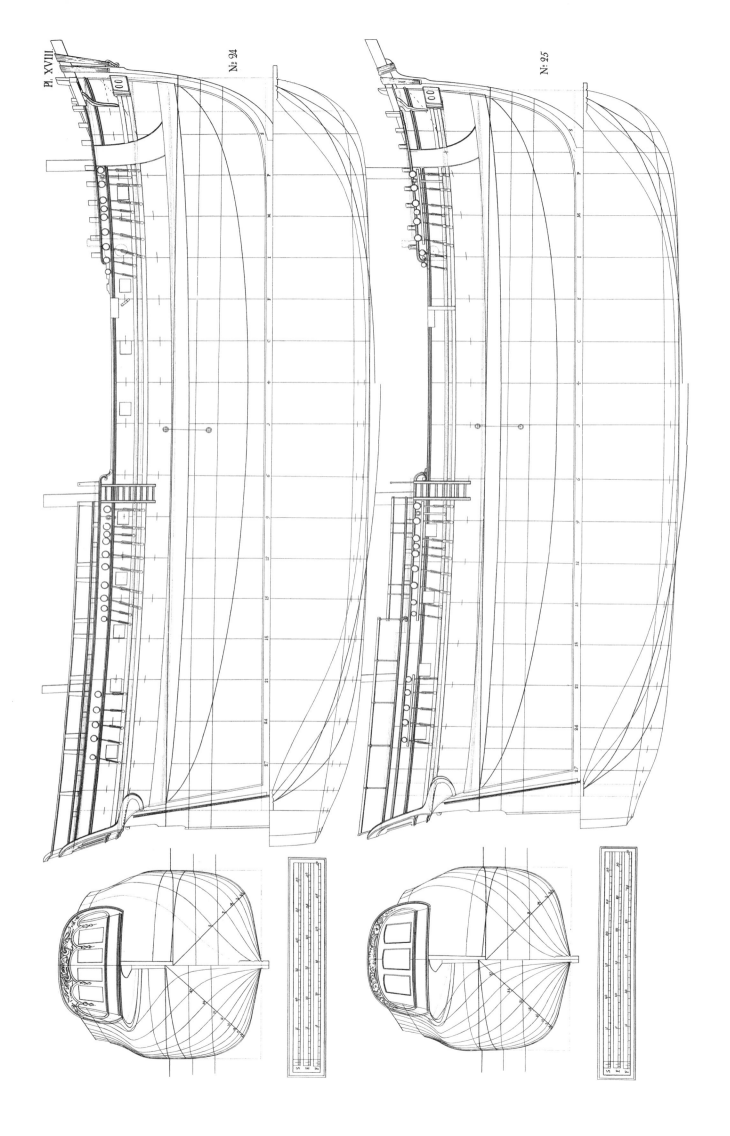

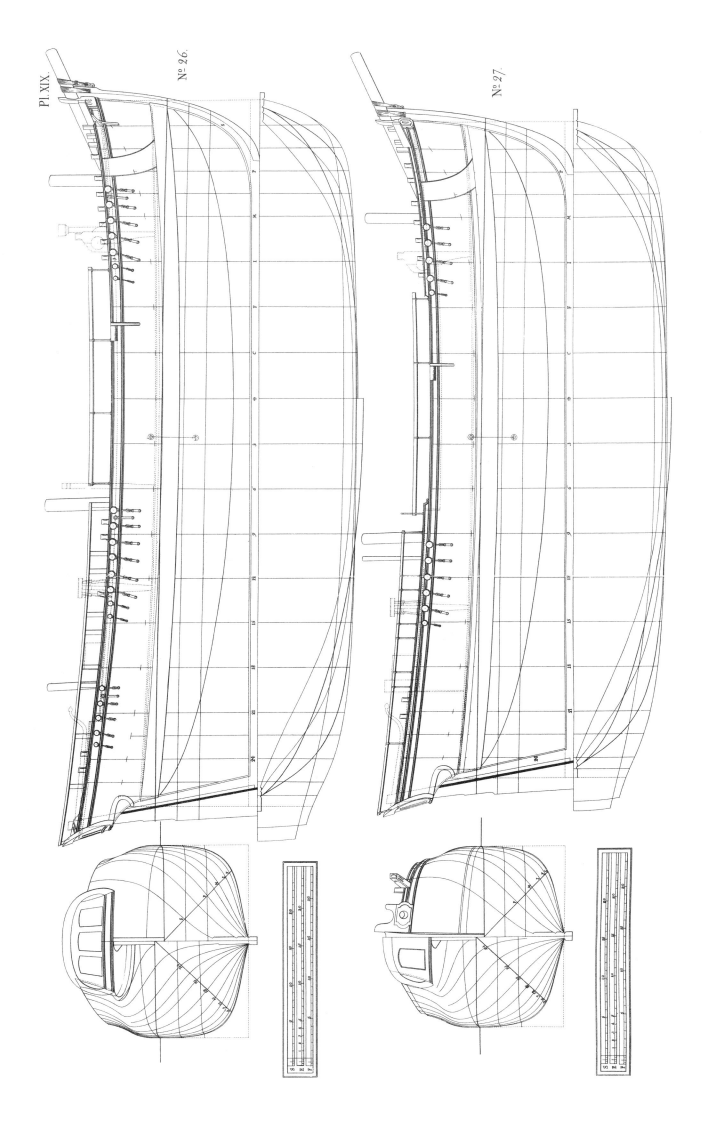

Pl. XIX.

Nº 26.

Nº 27.

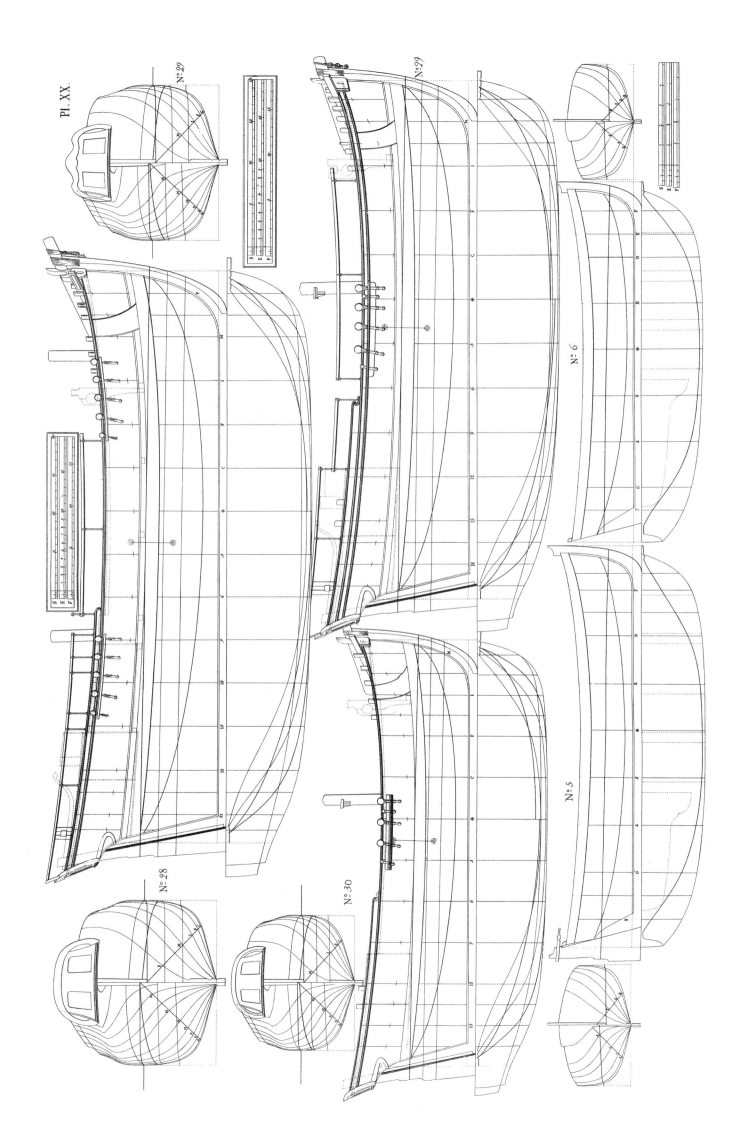

Pl. XX.

N° 29

N° 28

N° 29

N° 30

N° 6

N° 5

Pl. XXI

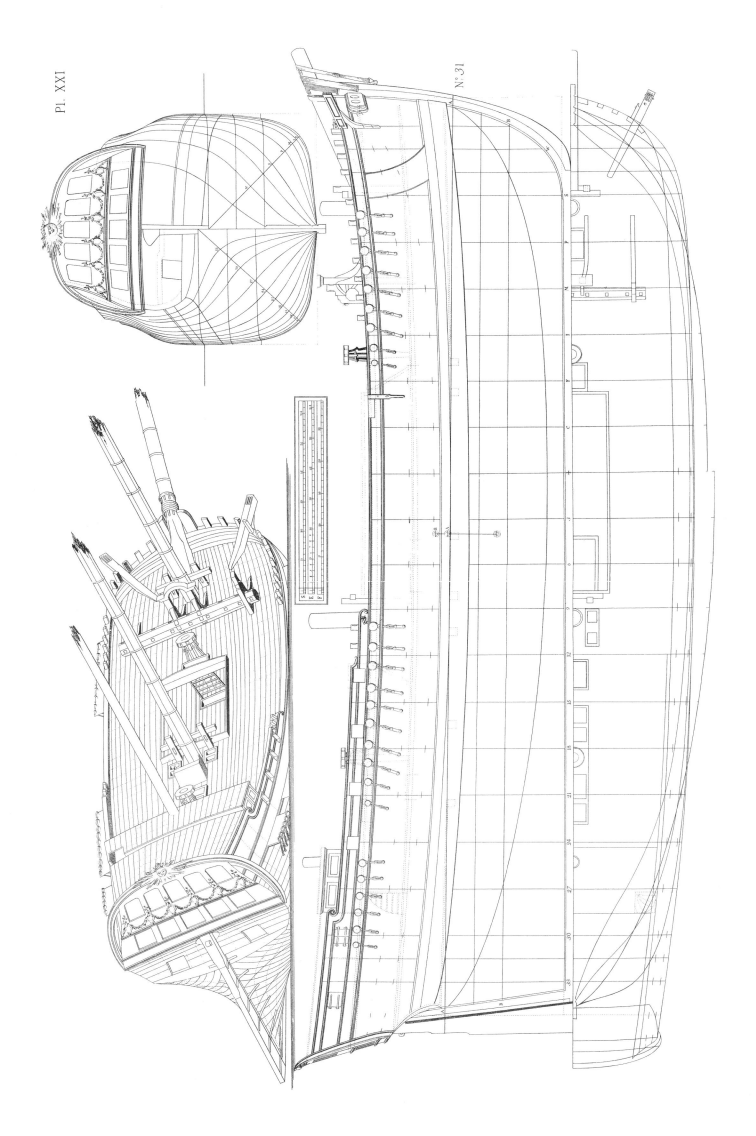

Pl. XXII.

N.º 32

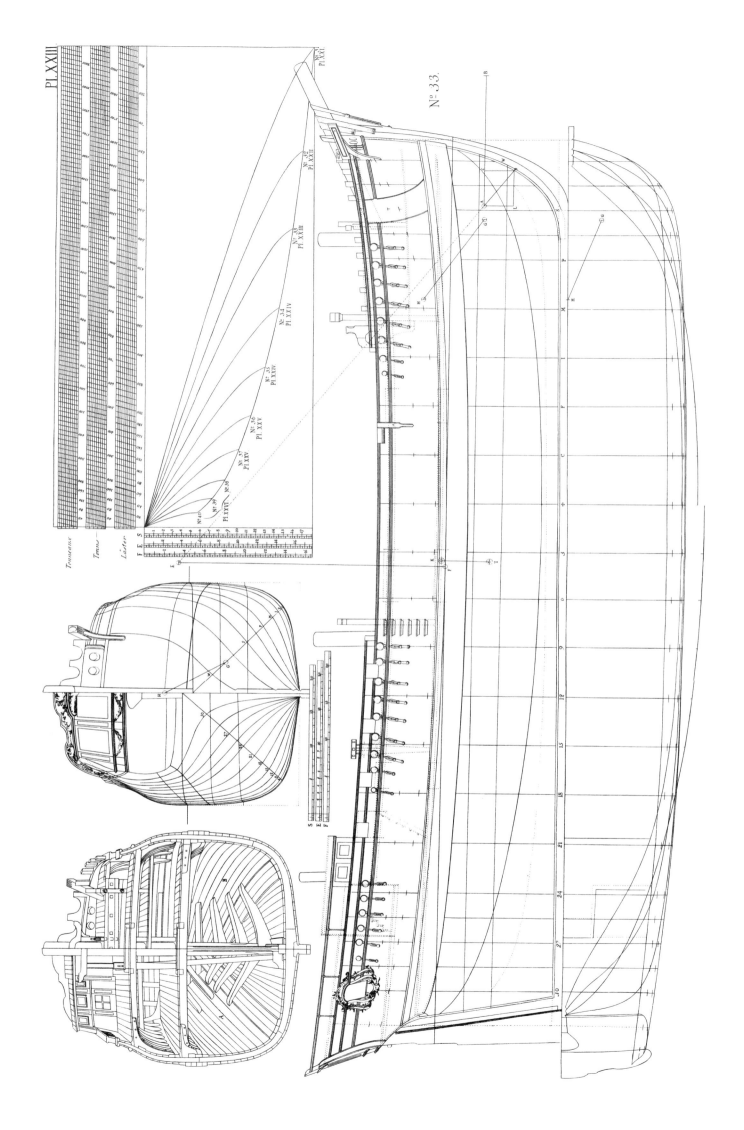

Pl. XXII

N.° 33.

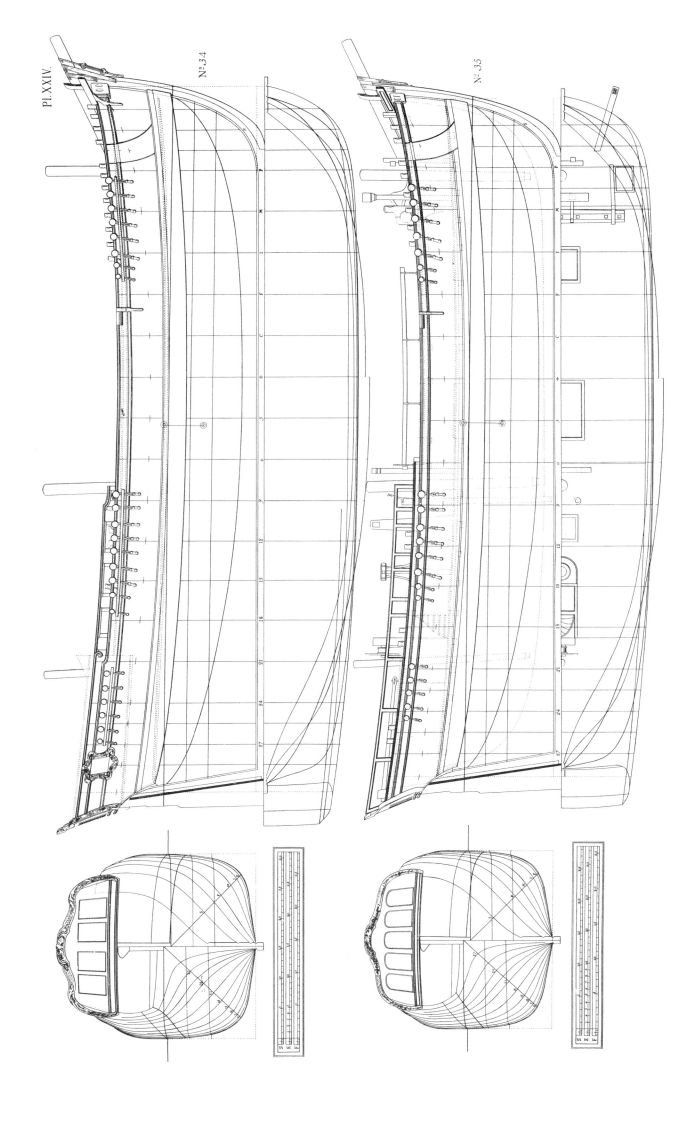

Pl. XXIV.

Nº 34

Nº 35

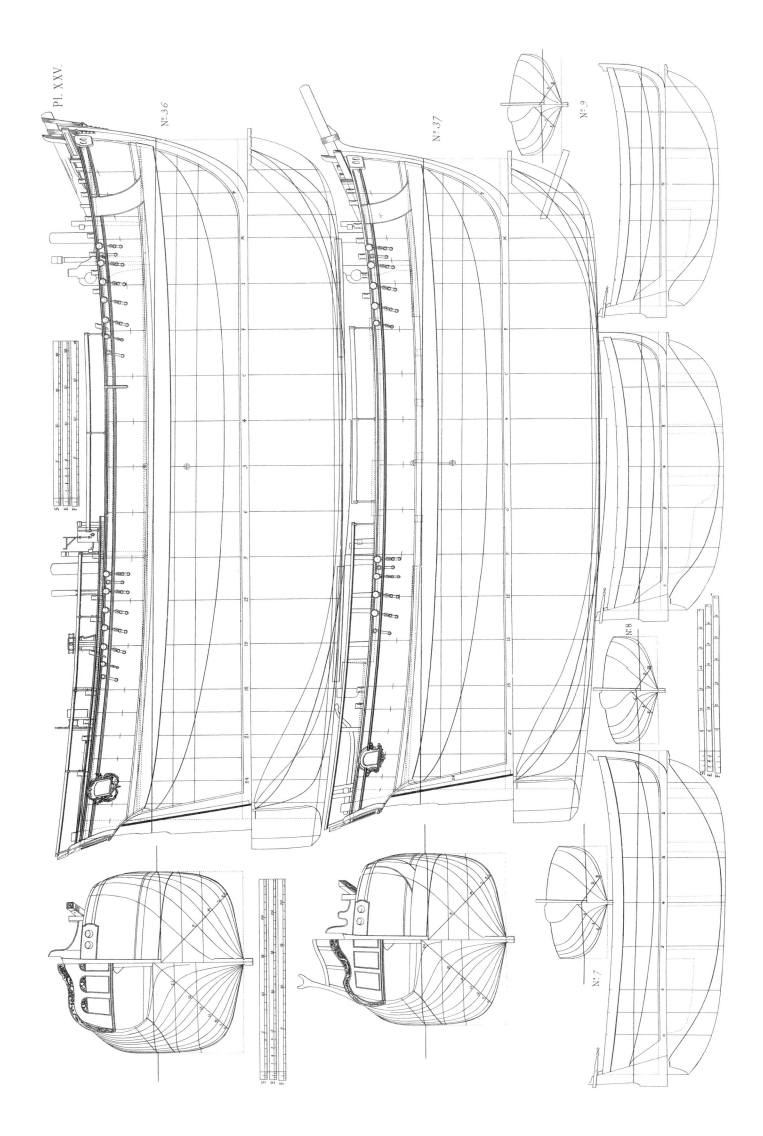

Pl. XXV.

N.º 36

N.º 37

N.º 9

N.º 8

N.º 7

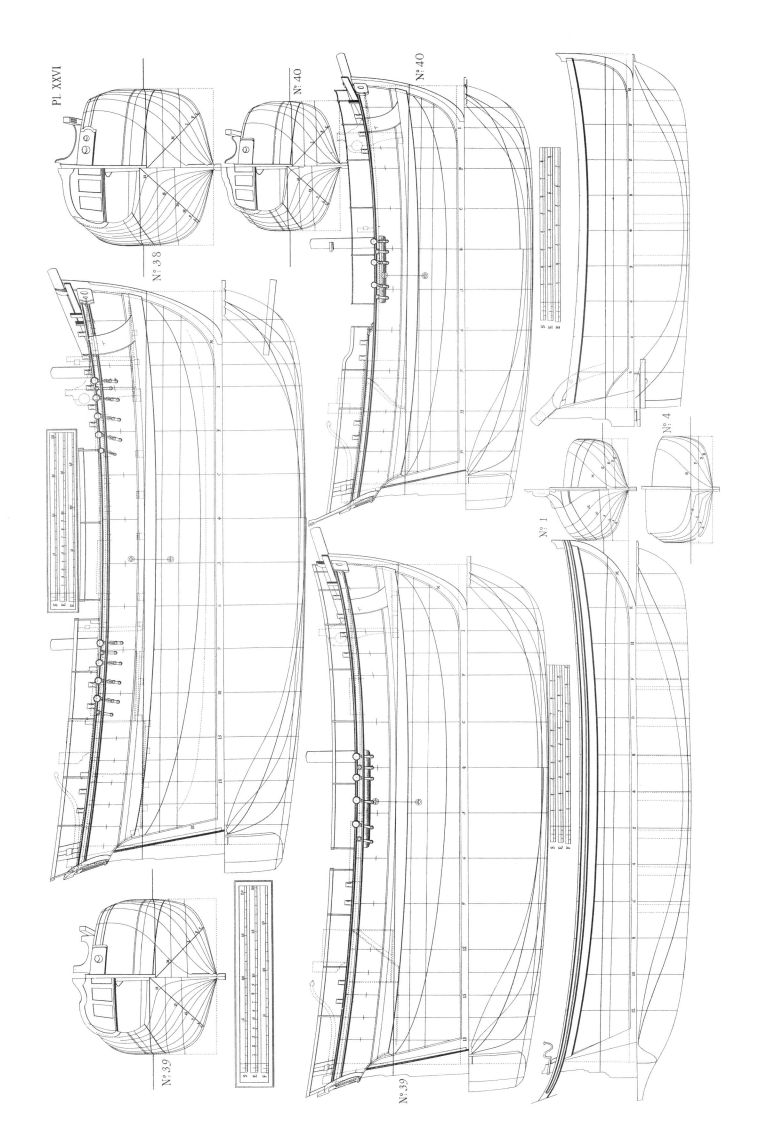

PL. XXVI

N.º 38

N.º 39

N.º 40

N.º 40

N.º 39

N.º 1

N.º 4

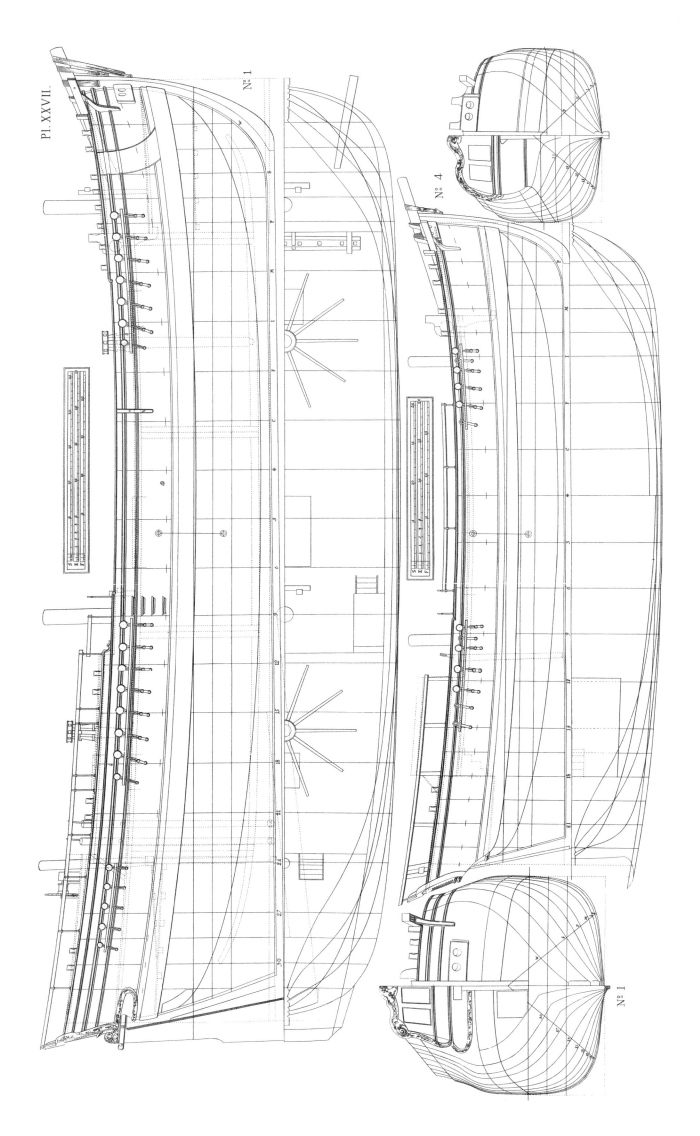

Pl. XXVII.

Nᵒ 1

Nᵒ 4

Nᵒ 1

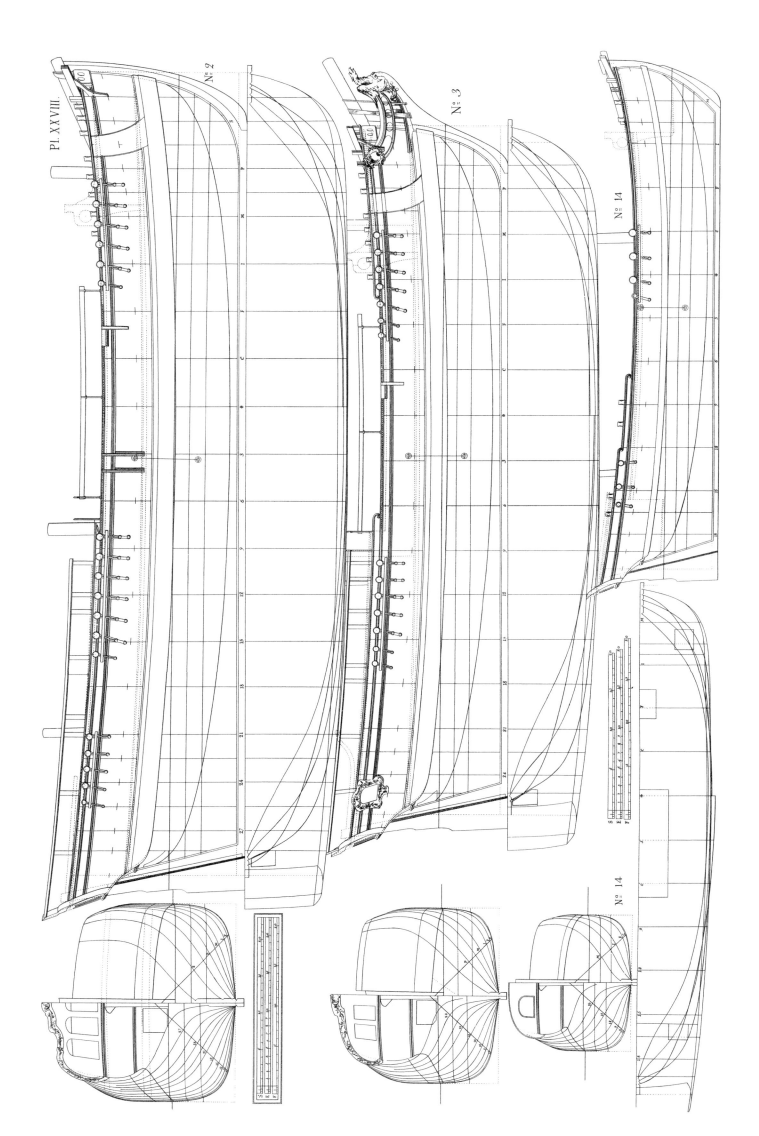

Pl. XXVIII.

N.º 2

N.º 3

N.º 14

N.º 14

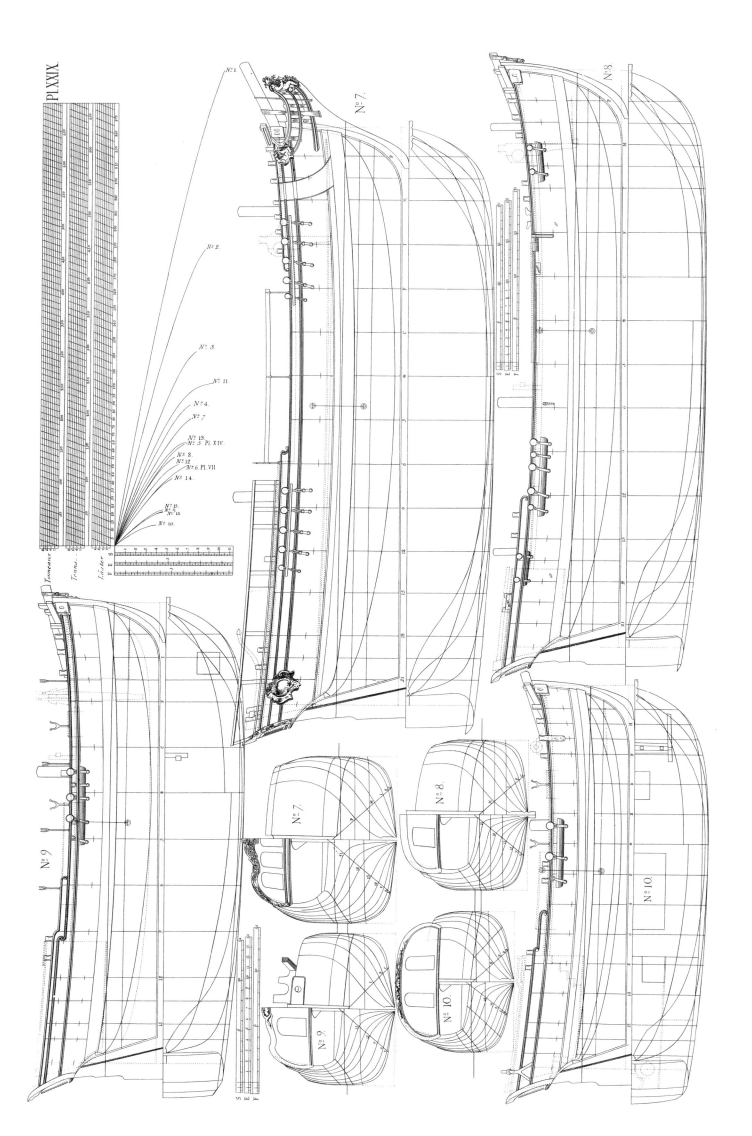

Pl. XXIX.

N.º 1.

N.º 2.

N.º 3.

N.º 11

N.º 4.
N.º 7
N.º 13
N.º 5 Pl. XIV.
N.º 8.
N.º 12
N.º 6. Pl.VII
N.º 14.

N.º 15.
N.º 9
N.º 15.
N.º 10.

N.º 7.

N.º 8.

N.º 9

N.º 7.

N.º 8.

N.º 10

N.º 9.

N.º 10.

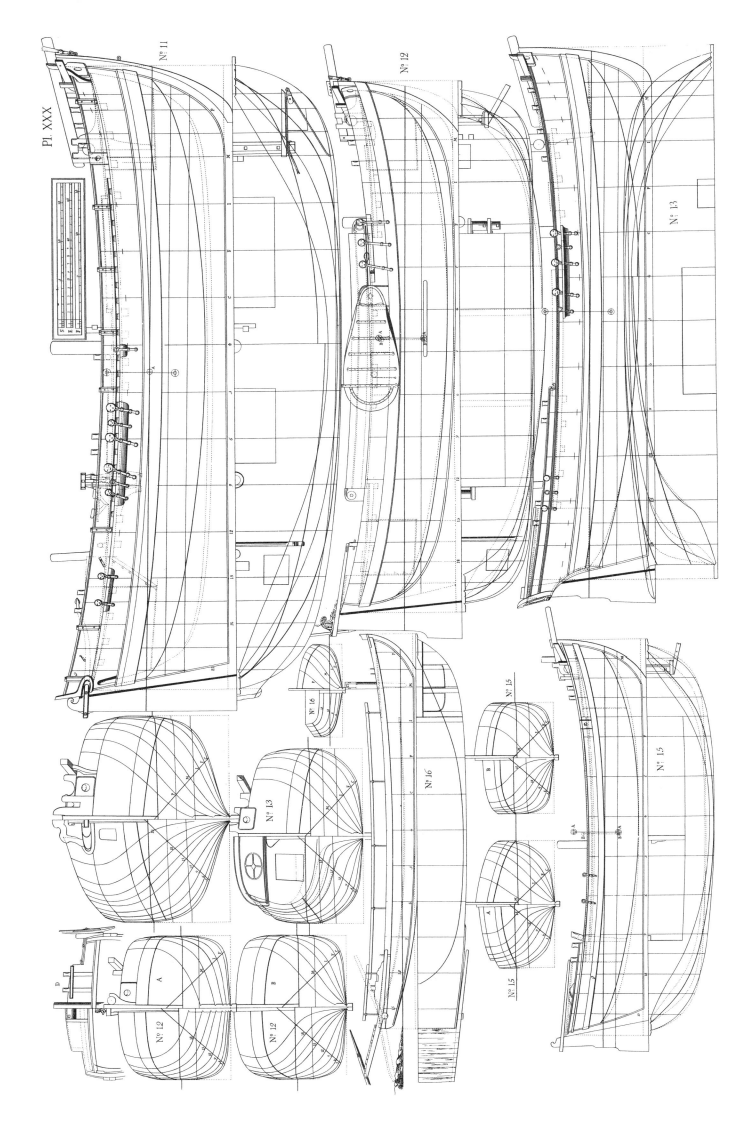

Pl. XXX

N.º 11

N.º 12

N.º 13

N.º 16

N.º 13

N.º 16

N.º 15

N.º 15

N.º 15

N.º 12

N.º 12

Pl. XXXI.

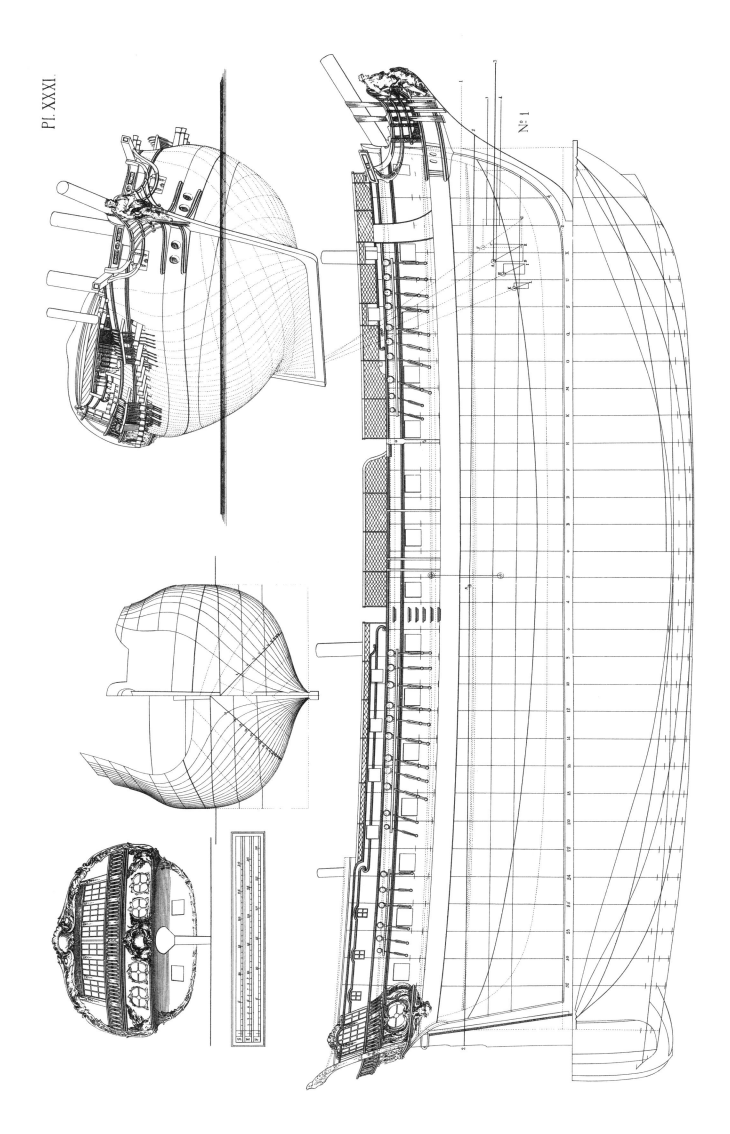

N.º 1

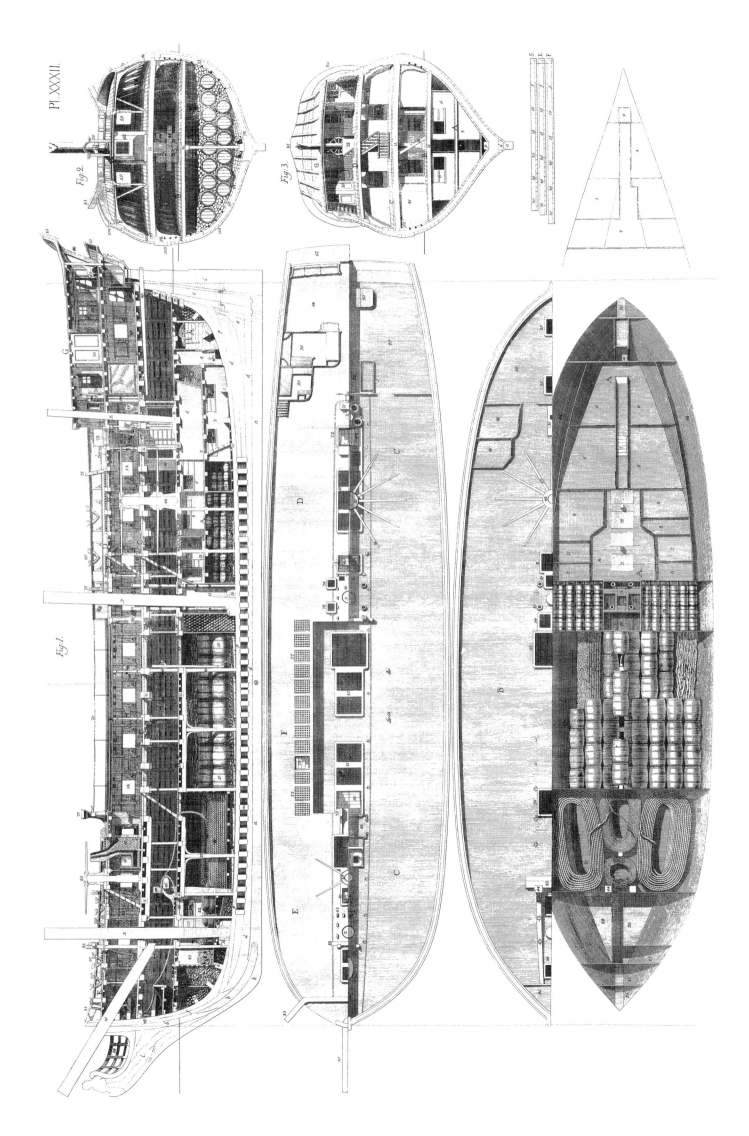

Pl. XXXII.

Fig. 1.

Fig. 2.

Fig. 3.

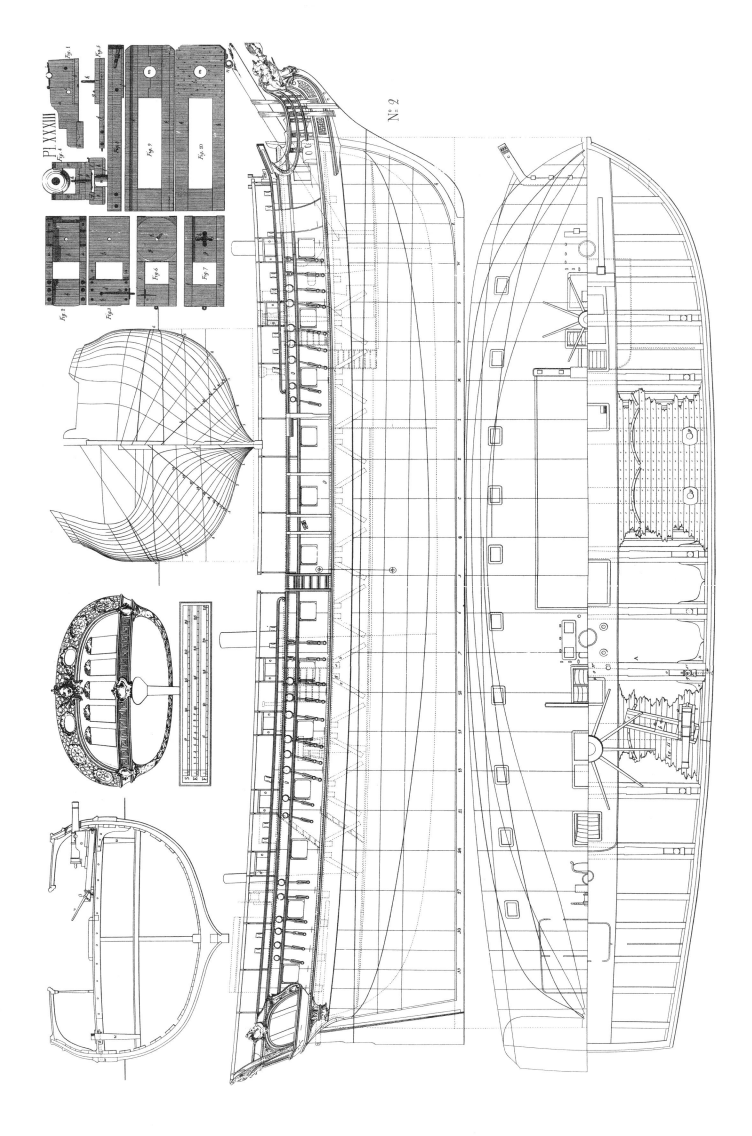

Pl. XXIII

Fig. 1
Fig. 5
Fig. 4
Fig. 8
Fig. 9
Fig. 10
Fig. 2
Fig. 3
Fig. 6
Fig. 7

N.º 2

Pl. XXIV

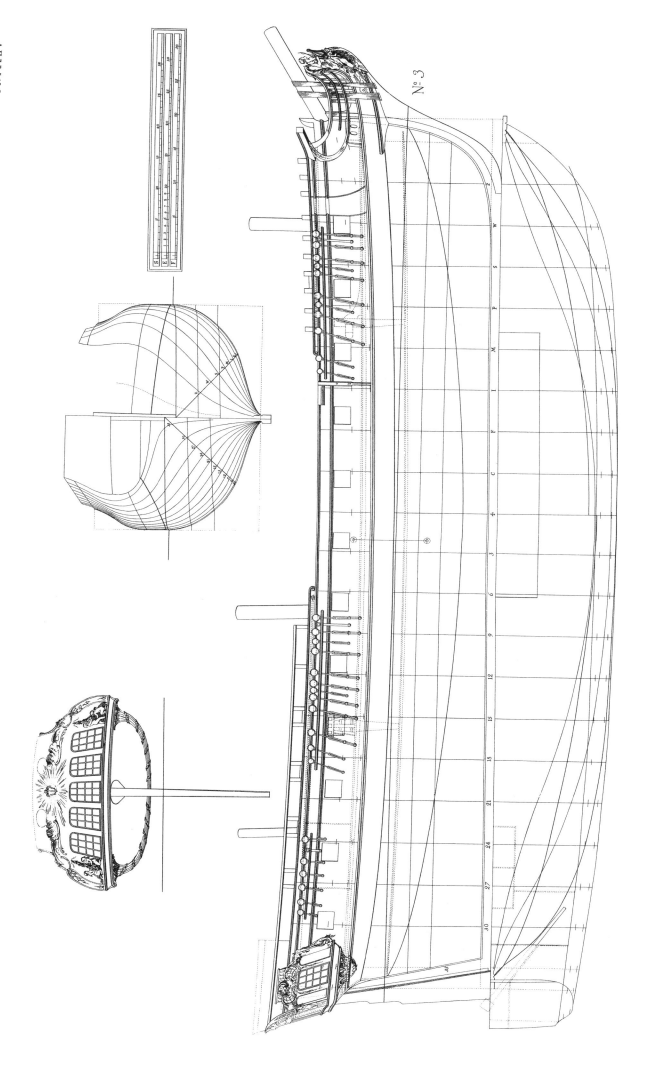

N.º 3

Pl. XXV.

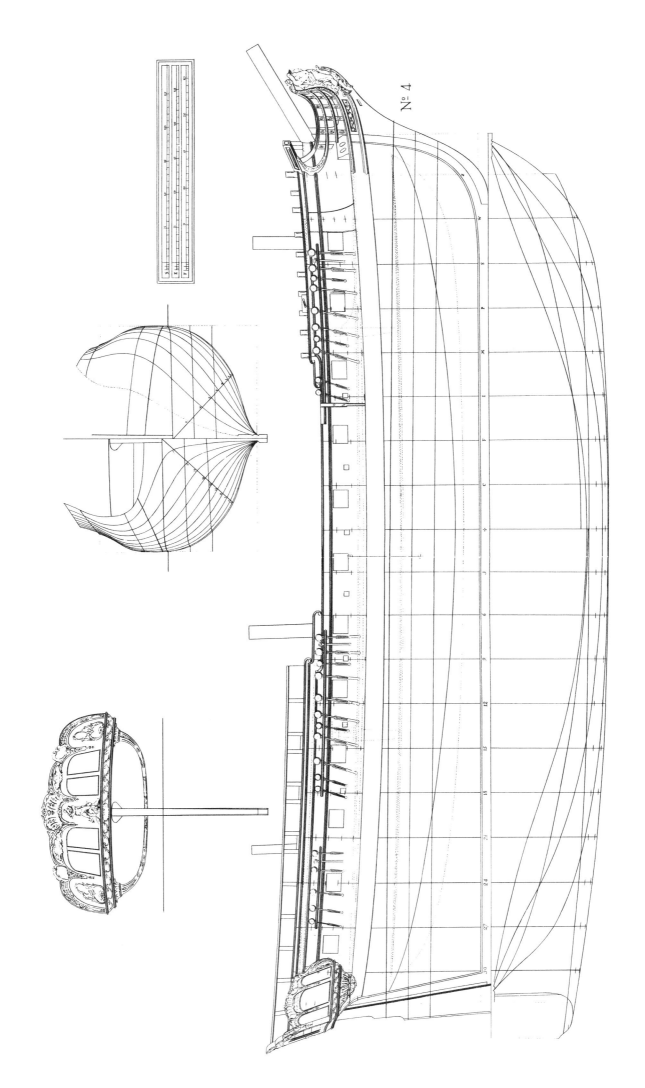

Nº 4

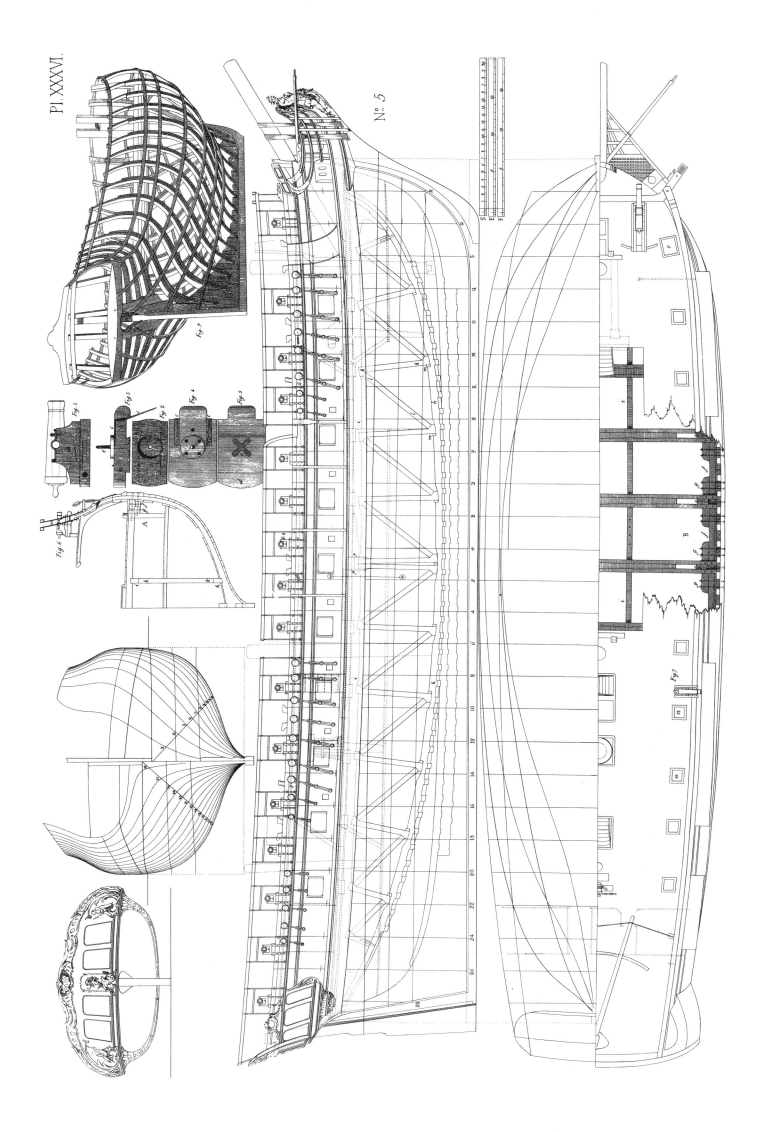

N.º 5

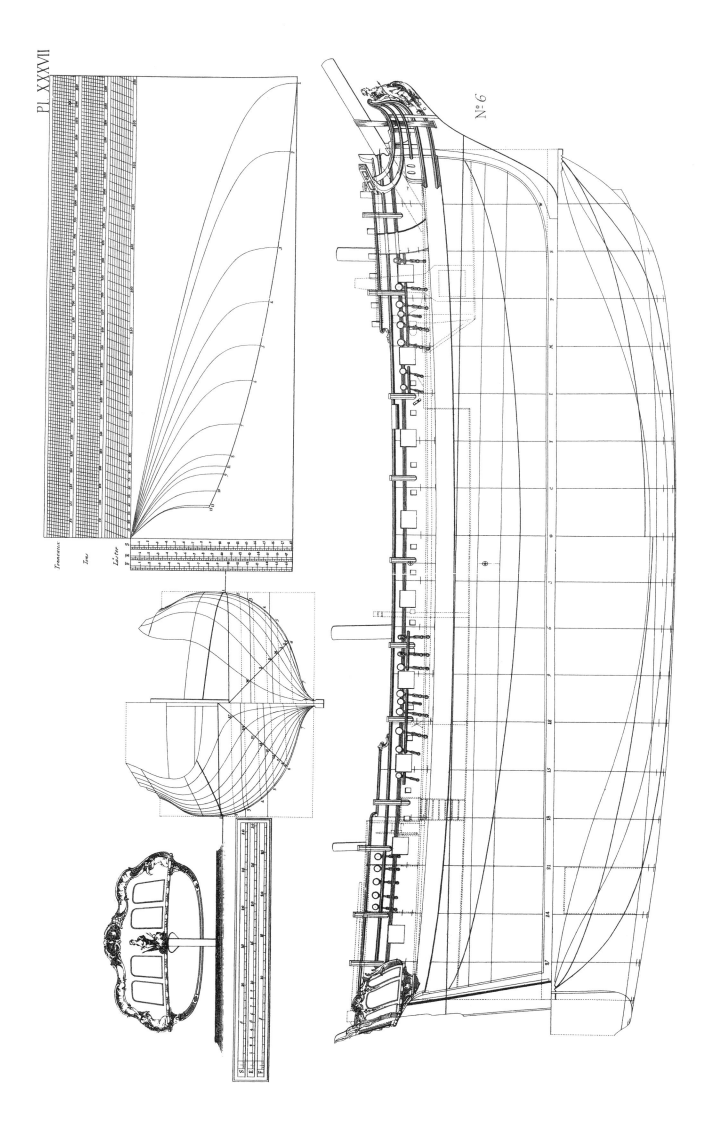

Pl. XXXVII

N.º 6

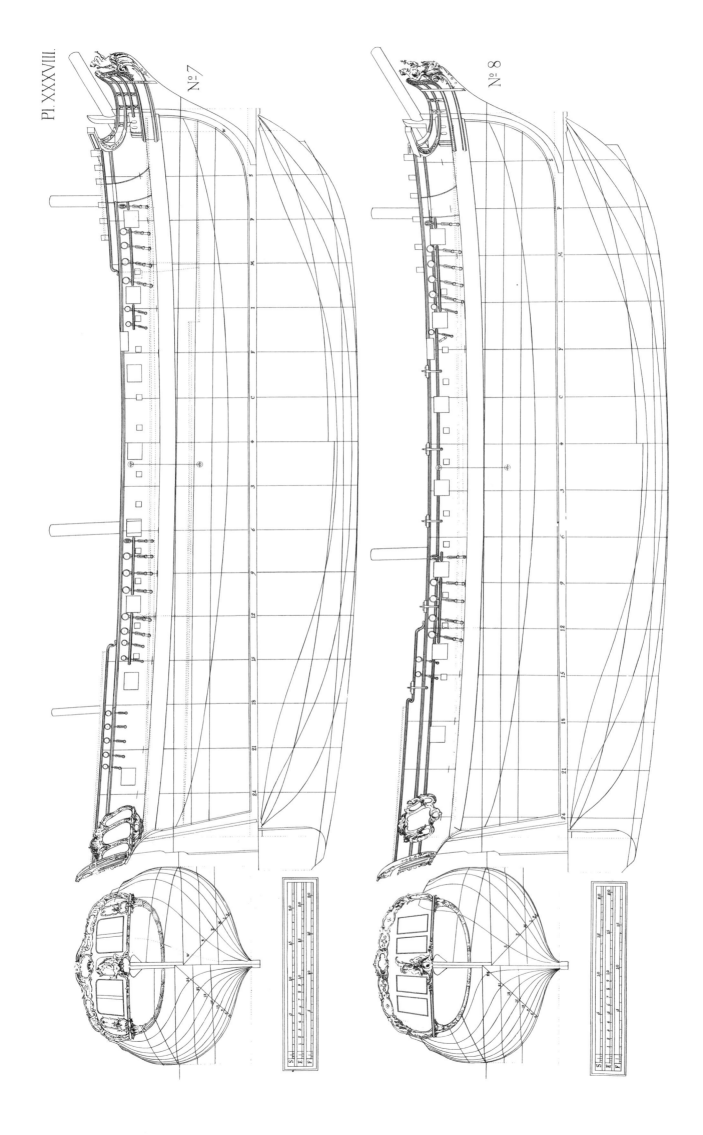

Pl. XXXVIII.

Nº 7

Nº 8

Pl. XXXIX.

N.º 9

N.º 10

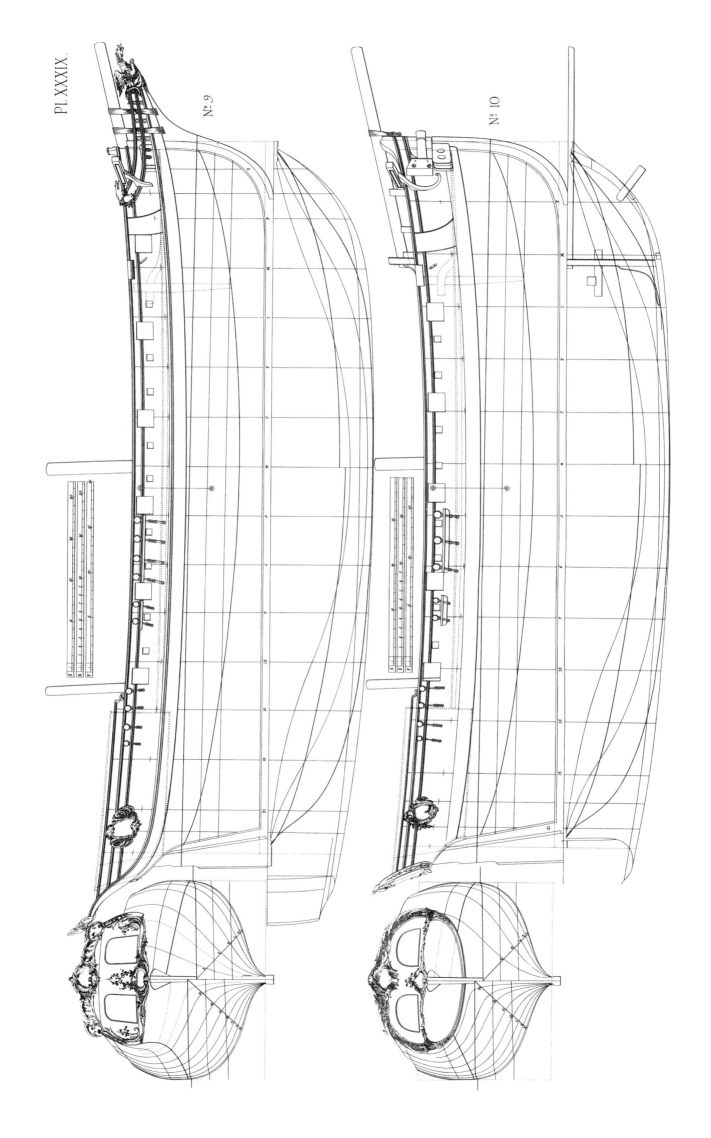

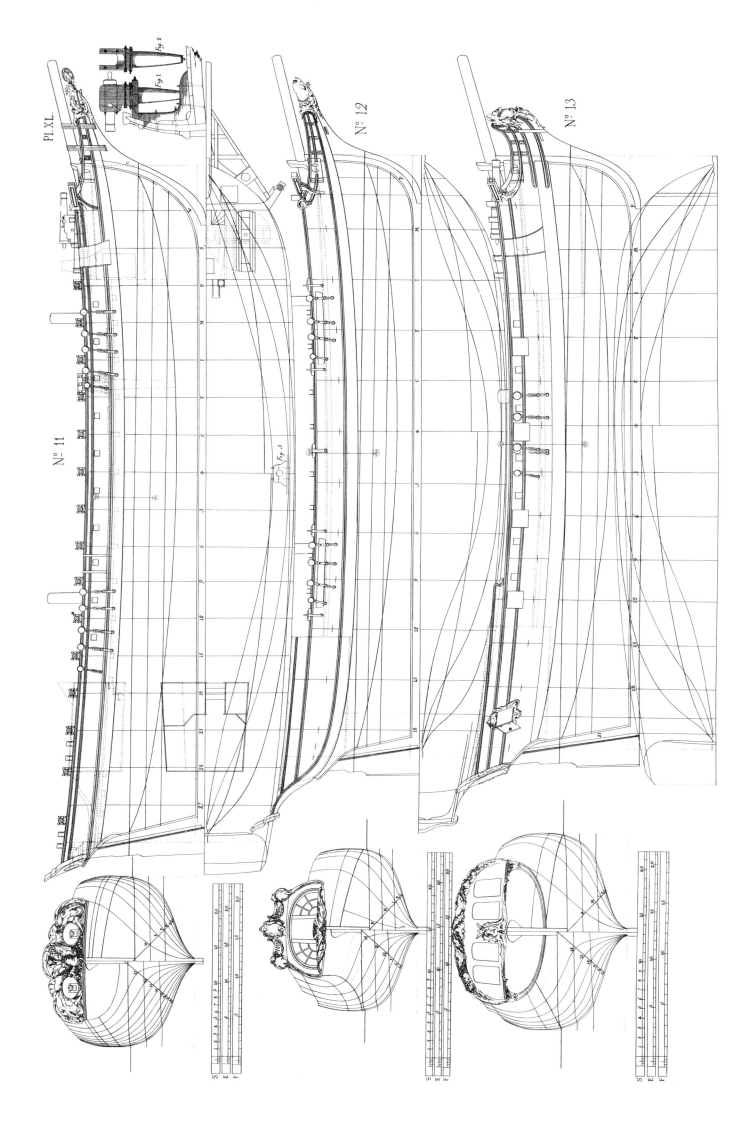

Pl. XL.

N° 11

N° 12

N° 13

Fig. 1
Fig. 2
Fig. 3

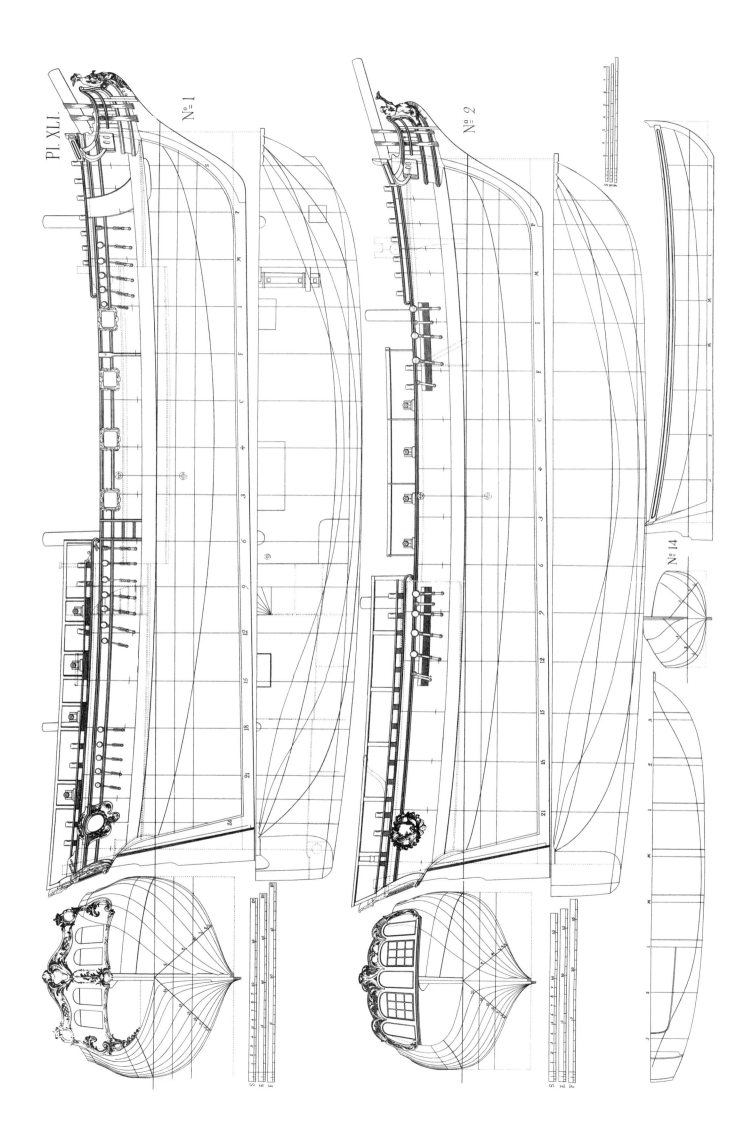

Pl. XLI.

N.º 1

N.º 2

N.º 14

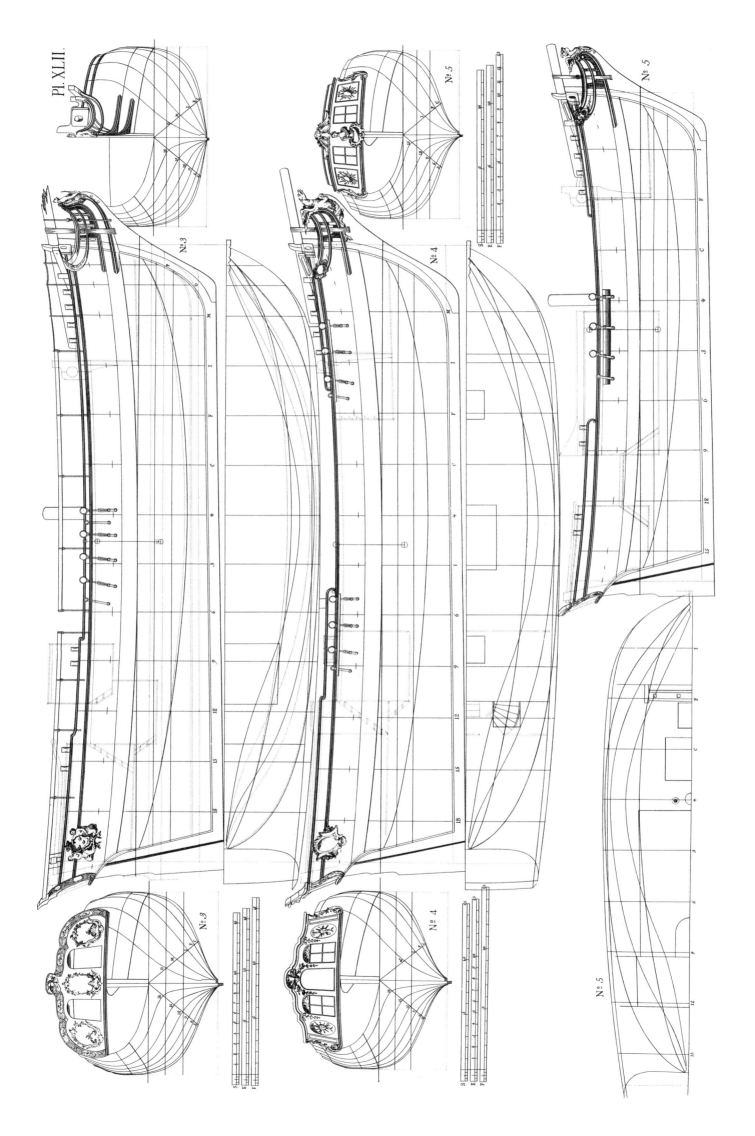

Pl. XLII.

N.º 3

N.º 4

N.º 5

N.º 3

N.º 4

N.º 5

Pl. XLIII

N°1

N° 2

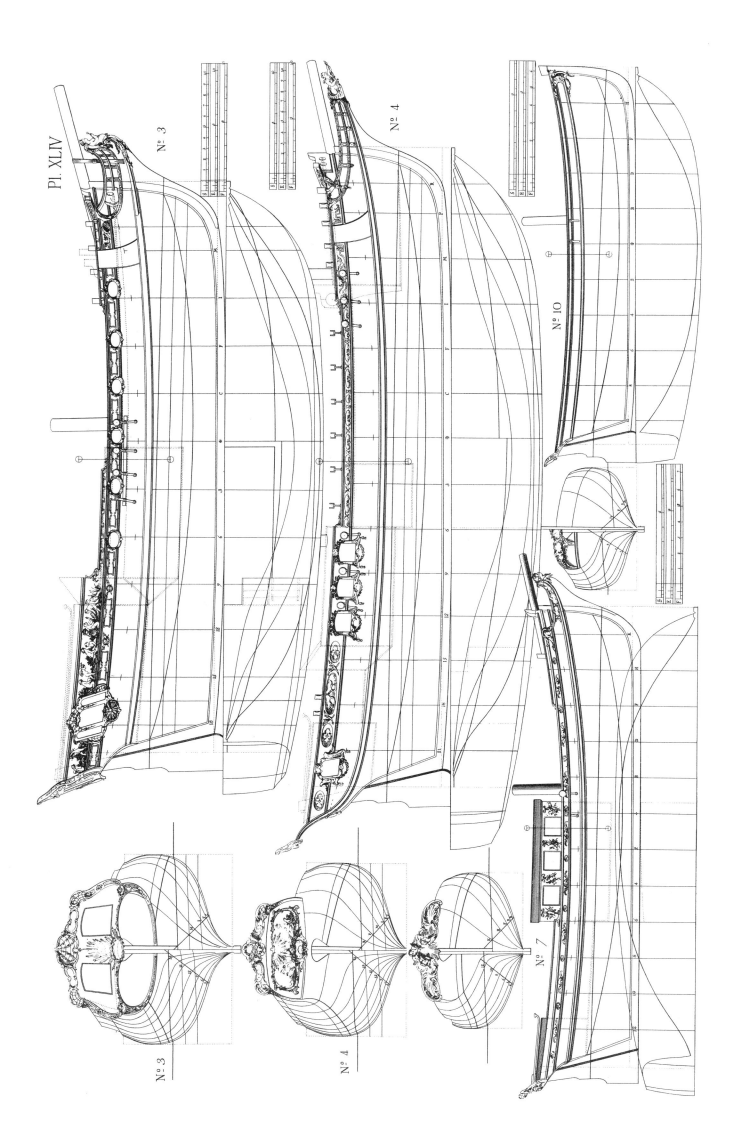

Pl. XLIV

Nᵒ 3

Nᵒ 4

Nᵒ IO

Nᵒ 7

Nᵒ 3

Nᵒ 4

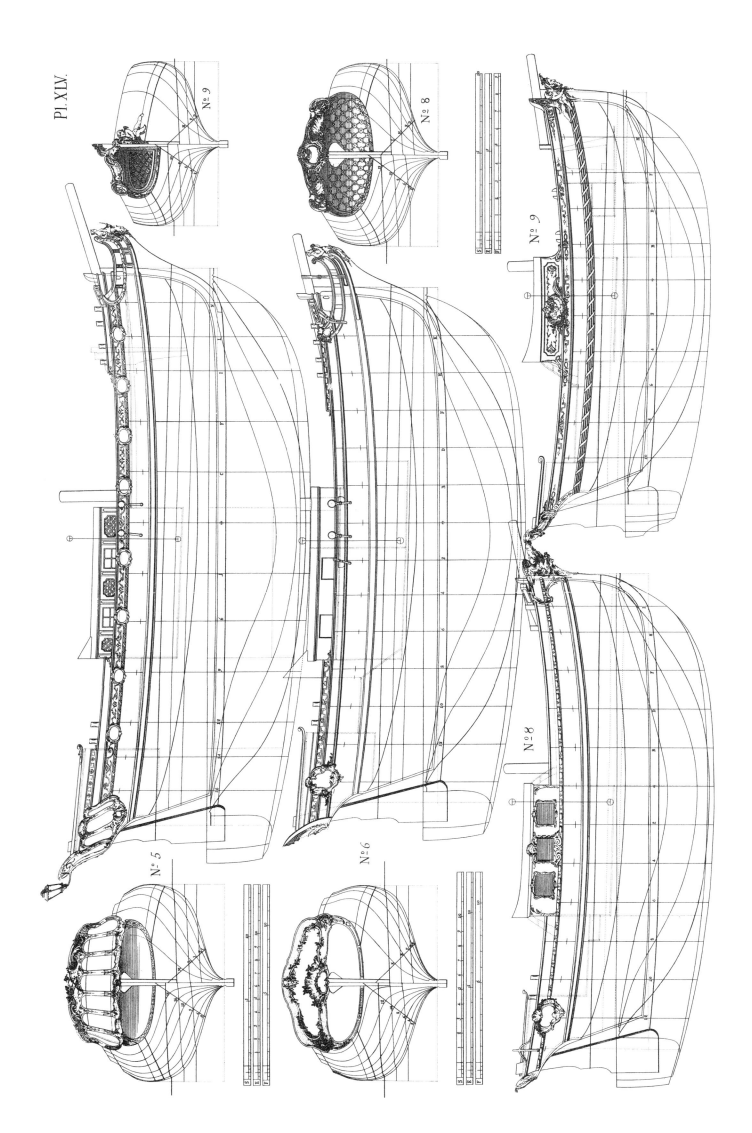

Pl. XLV.

Nº 9

Nº 8

Nº 9

Nº 5

Nº 6

Nº 8

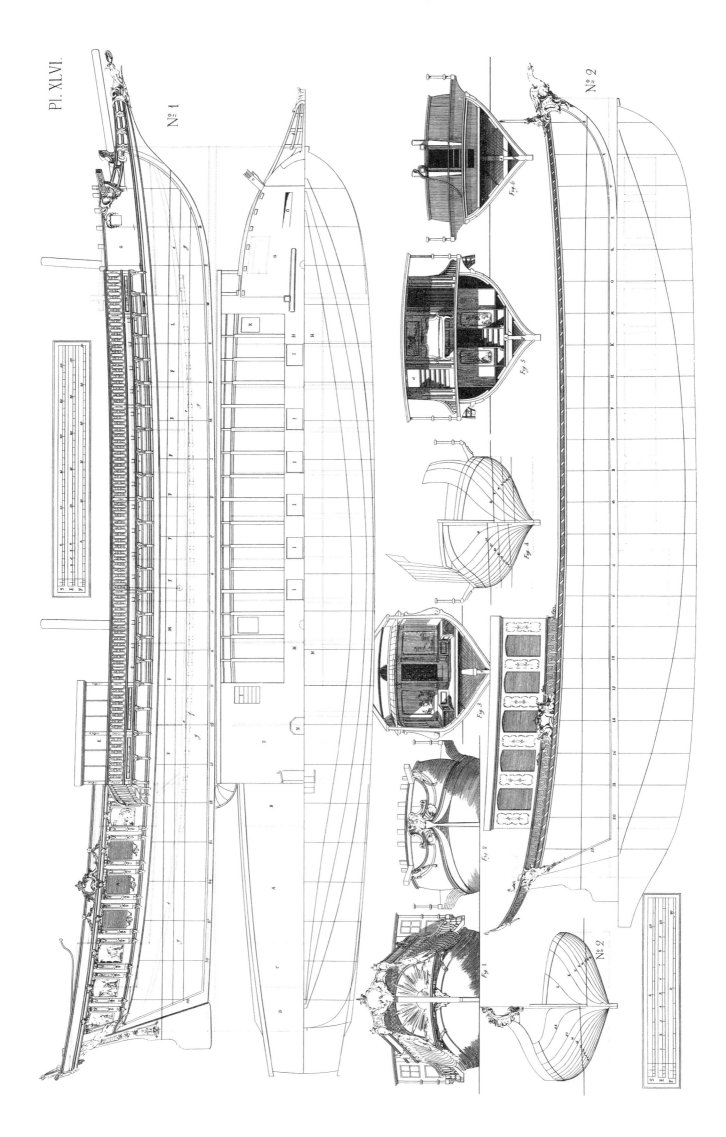

Pl. XLVI.

N.º 1

N.º 2

Fig. 6

Fig. 5

Fig. 4

Fig. 3

Fig. 2

Fig. 1

N.º 2

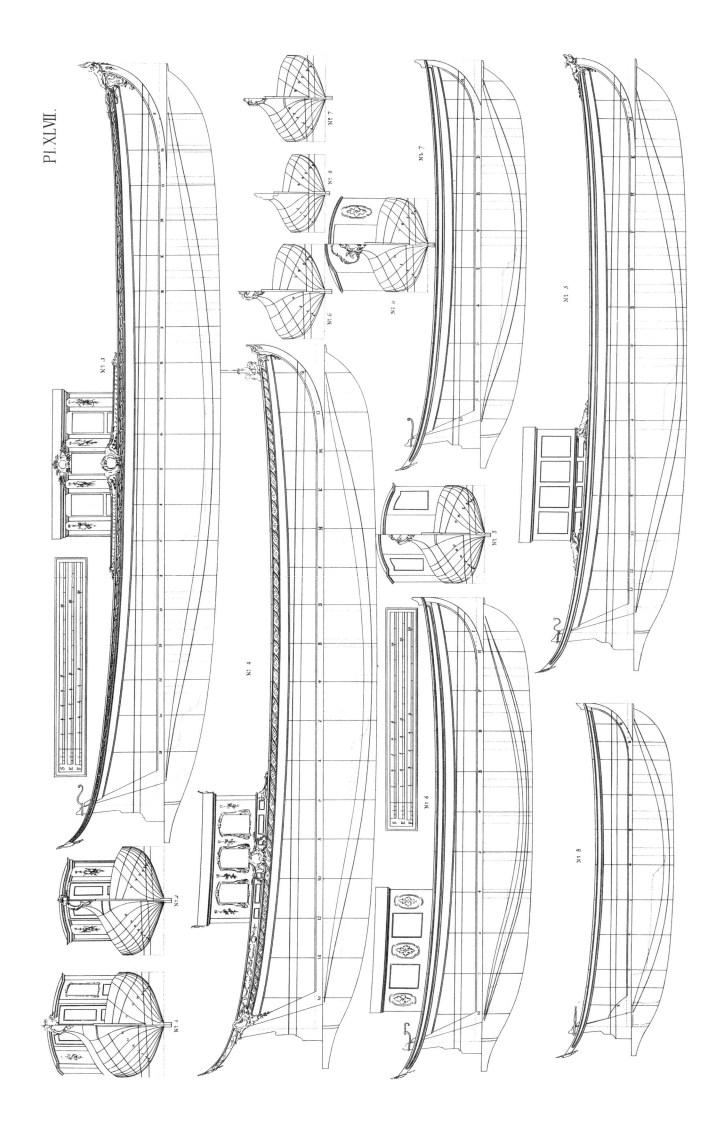

Pl. XLVII.

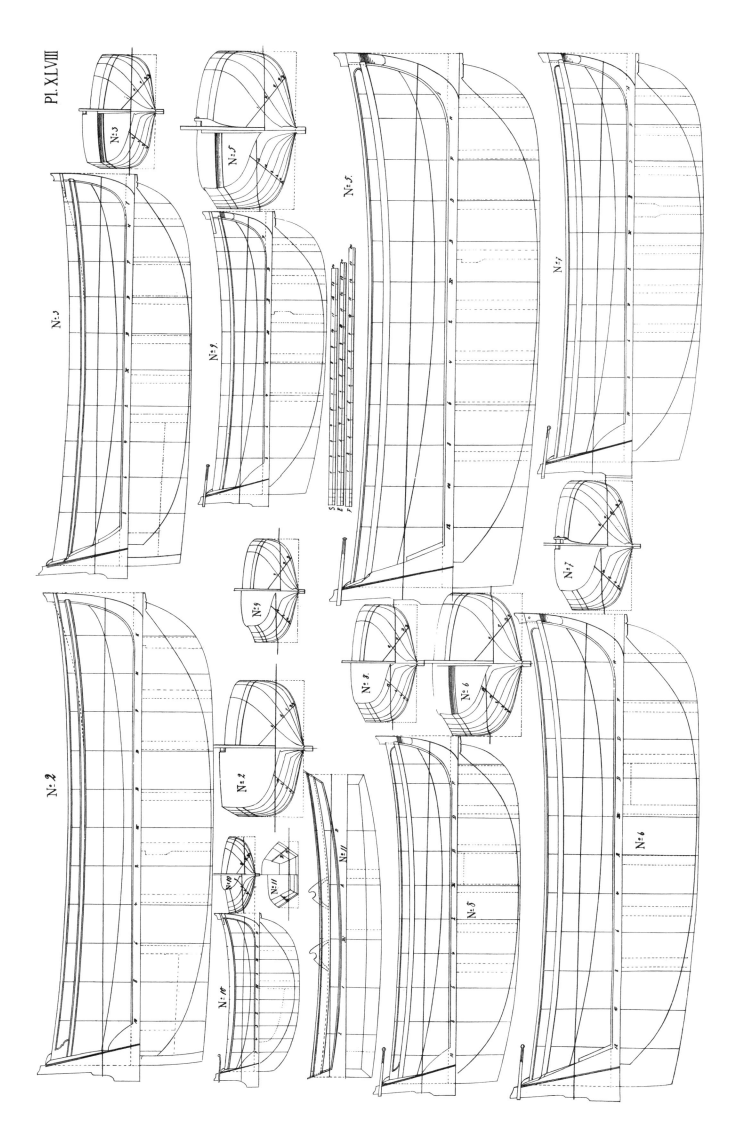

Pl. XLVIII

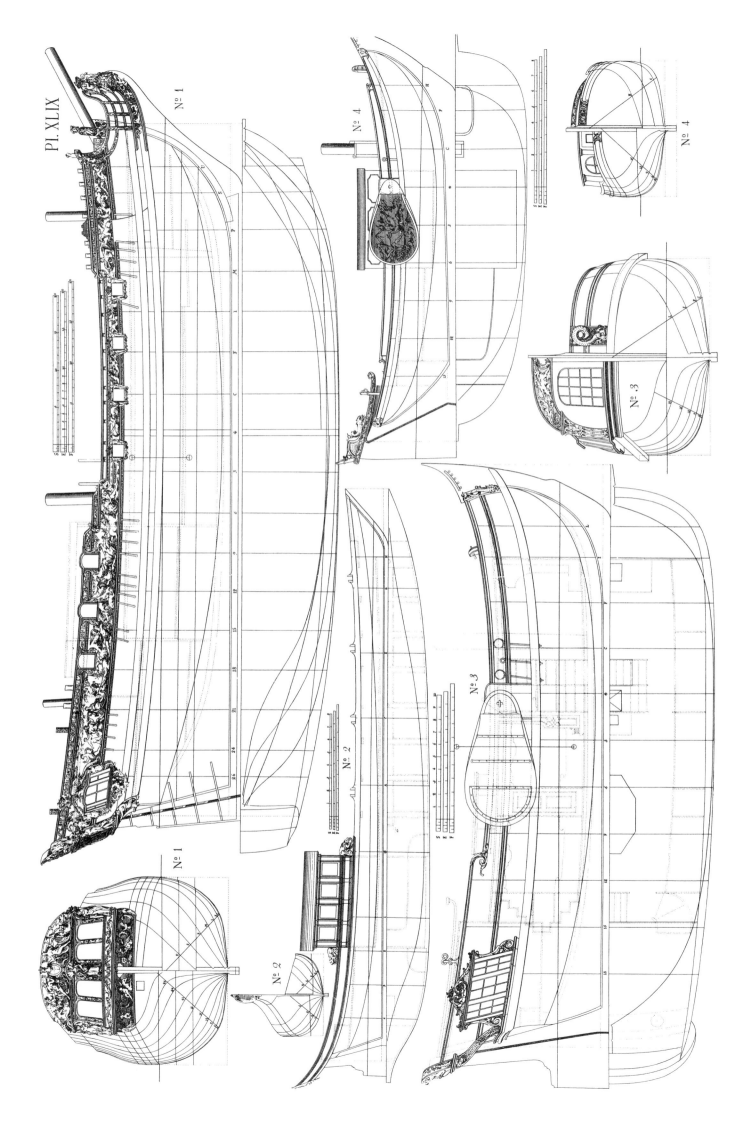

Pl. XLIX

Nº 1

Nº 4

Nº 4

Nº 3

Nº 1

Nº 2

Nº 3

Nº 2

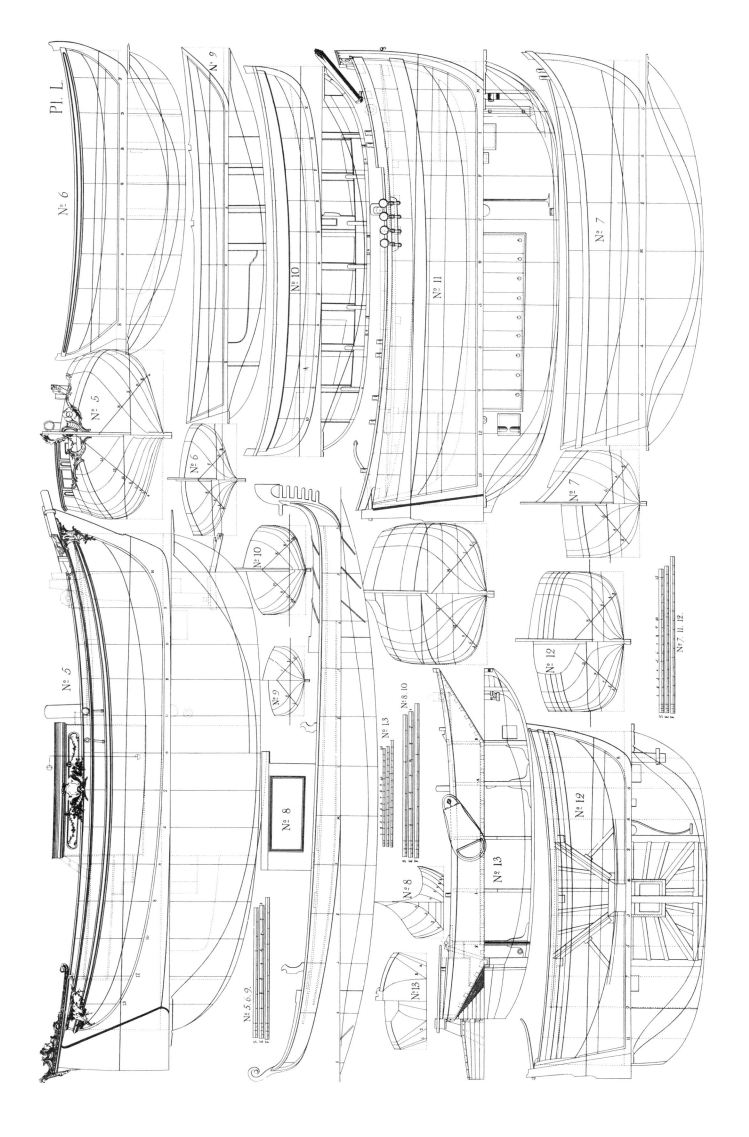

Pl. I.

Pl. LI.

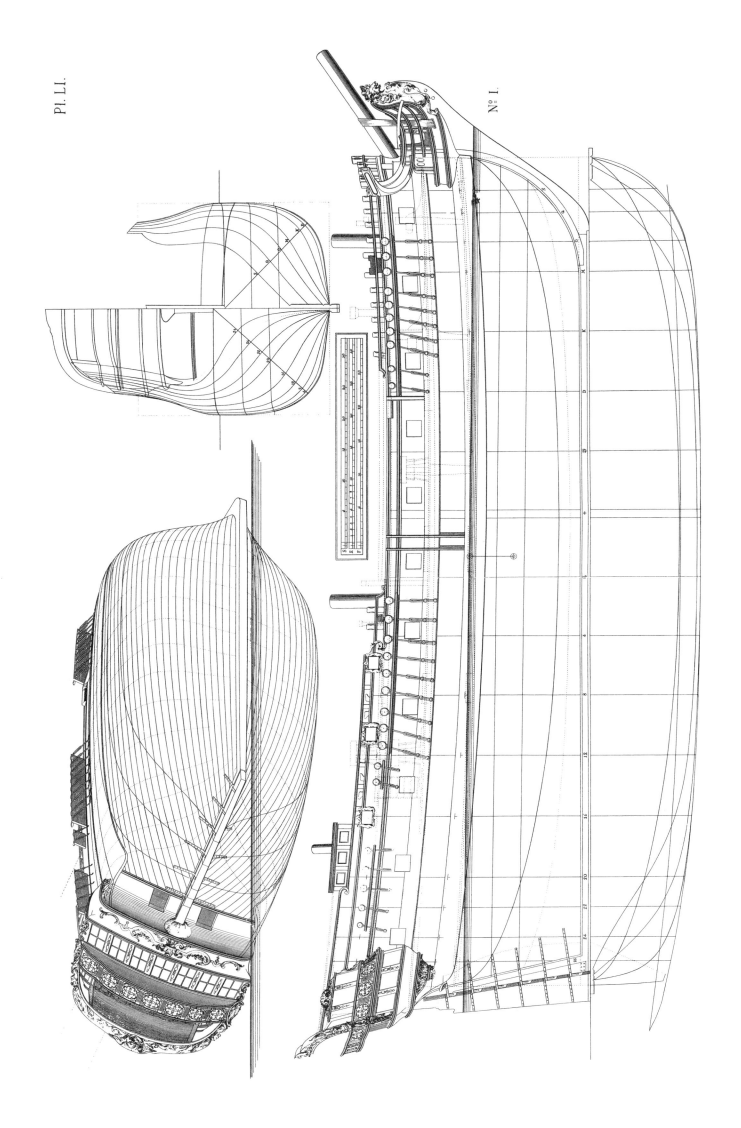

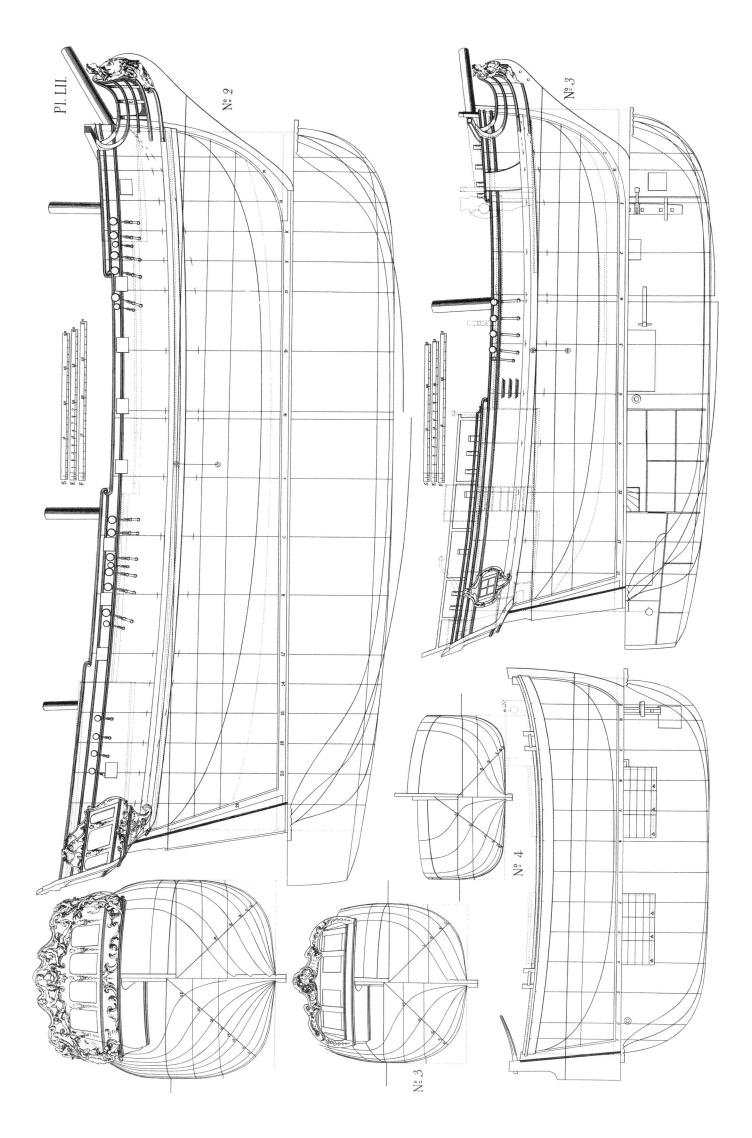

Pl. LII.

N° 2

N° 3

N° 4

N° 3

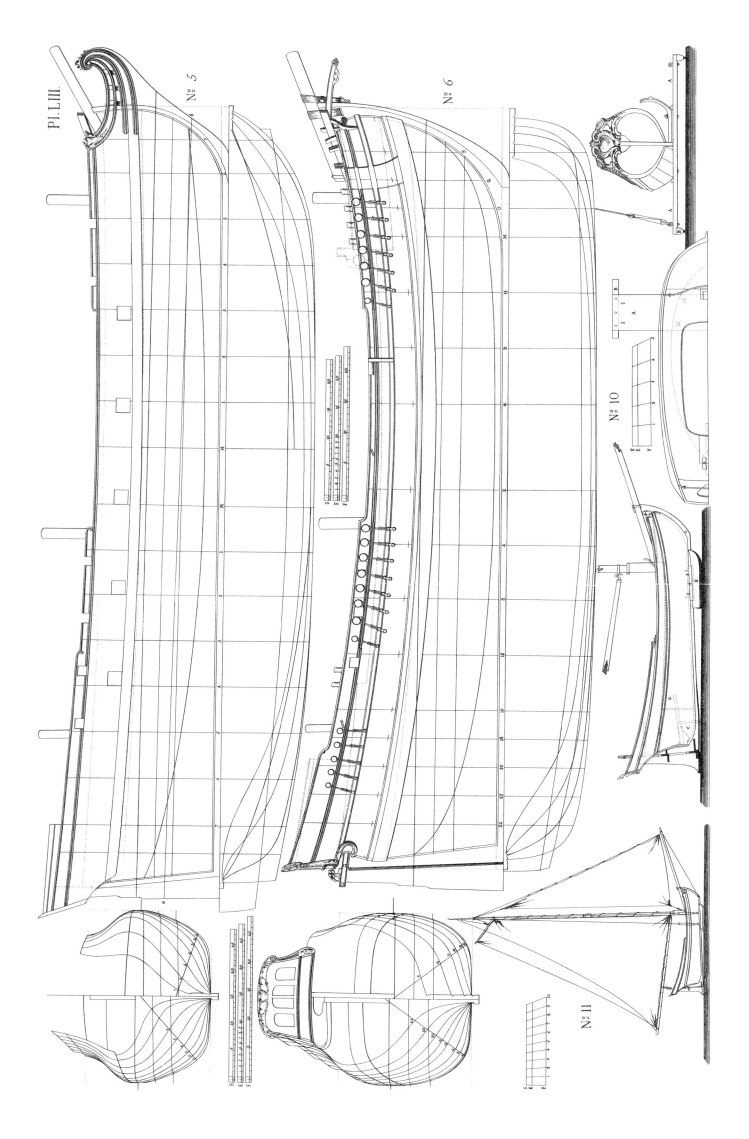

Pl. LIII.

Nº 5

Nº 6

Nº 10

Nº 11

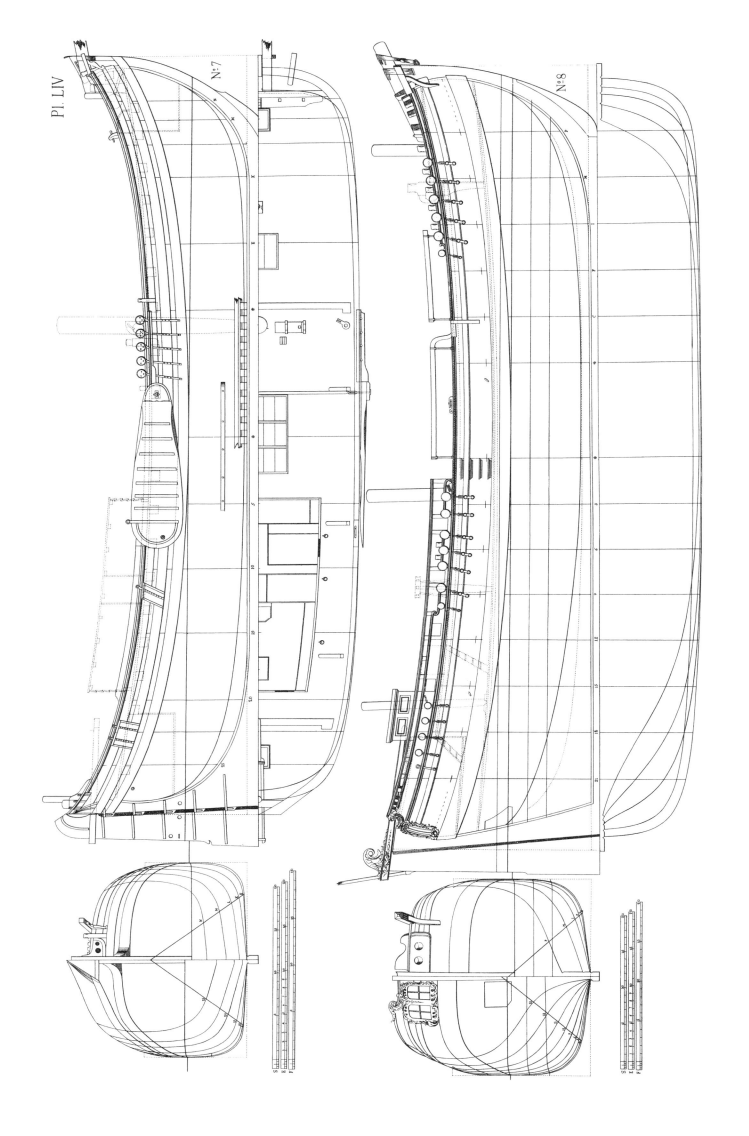

Pl. LIV

N° 7

N° 8

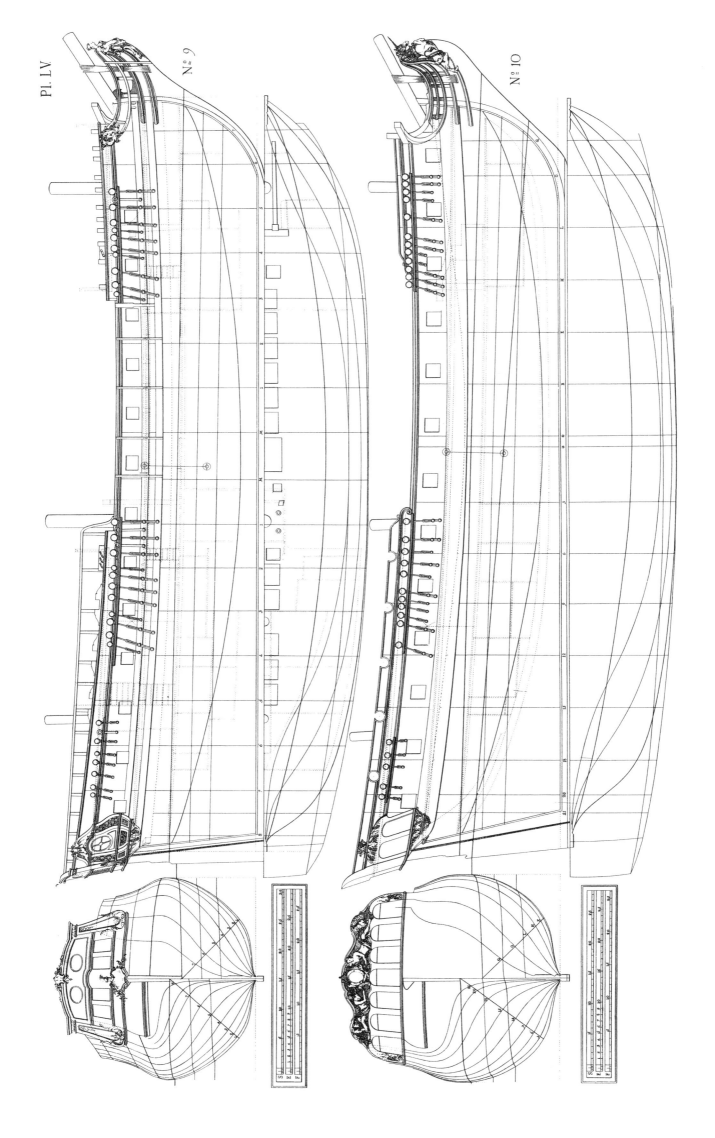

Pl. LV

N.º 9

N.º 10

Pl. LVI.

N.º 11

N.º 12

N.º 19

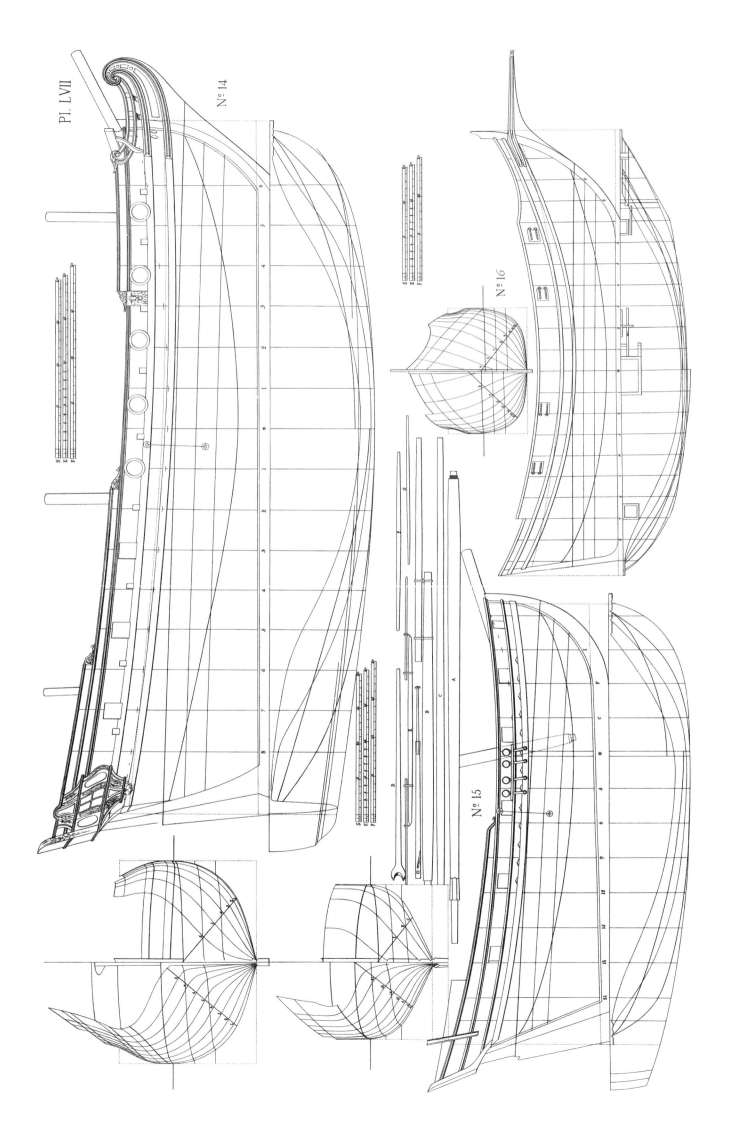

Pl. LVII

Nº 14

Nº 15

Nº 16

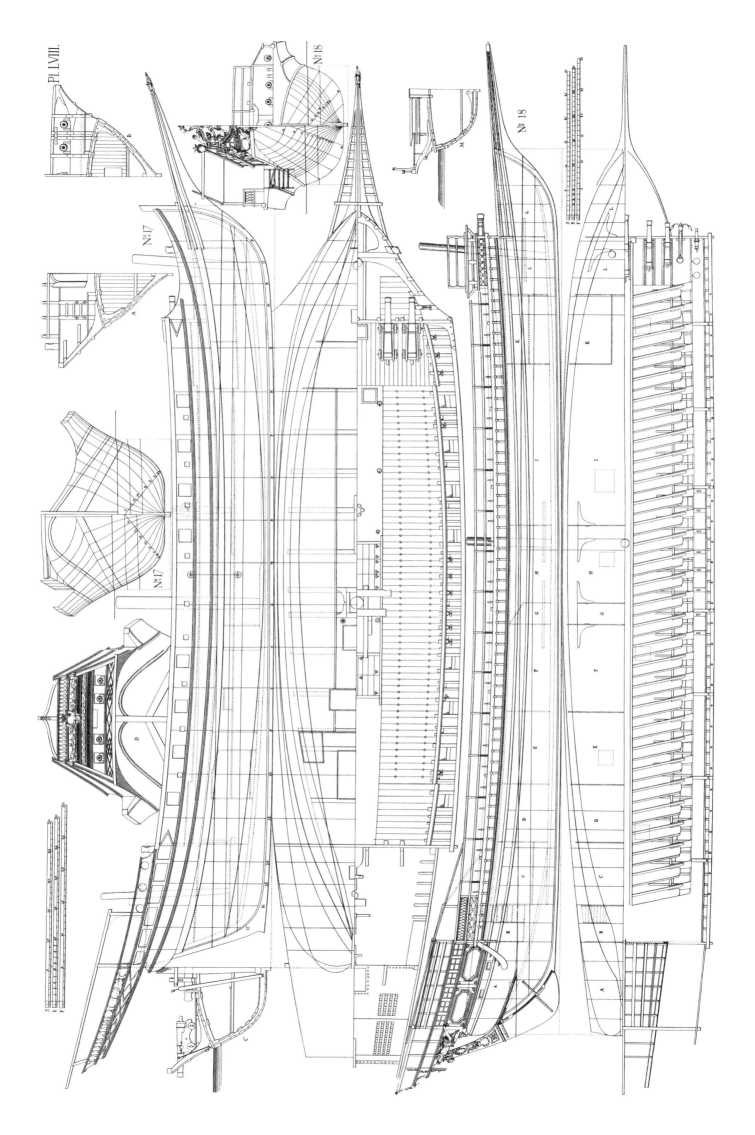

Pl. LVIII.

Nᵒ 18

Nᵒ 17

Nᵒ 18

Nᵒ 17

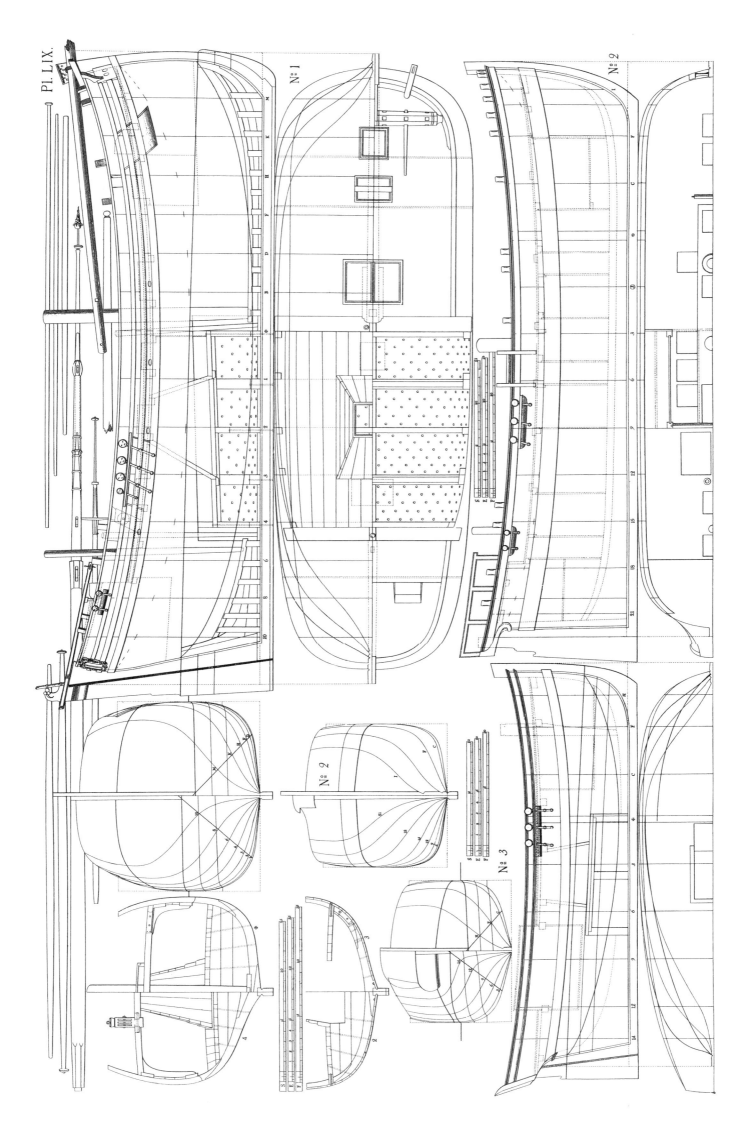

Pl. LIX.

Nº 1

Nº 2

Nº 2

Nº 3

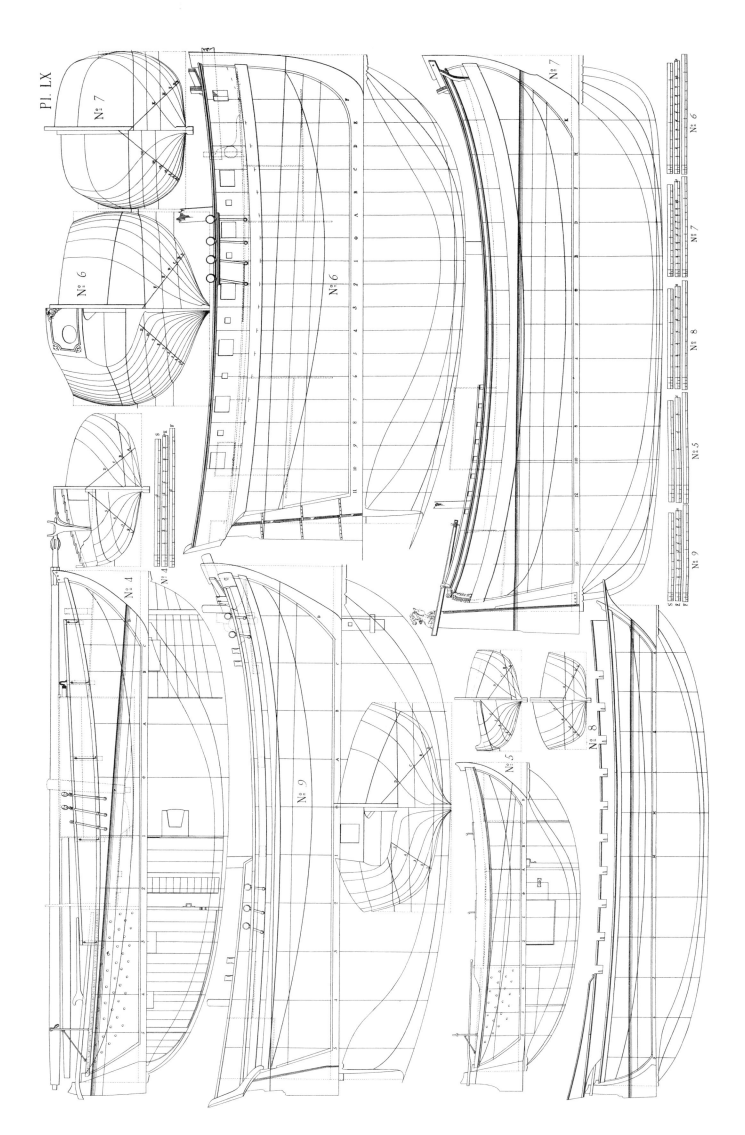

Pl. LX

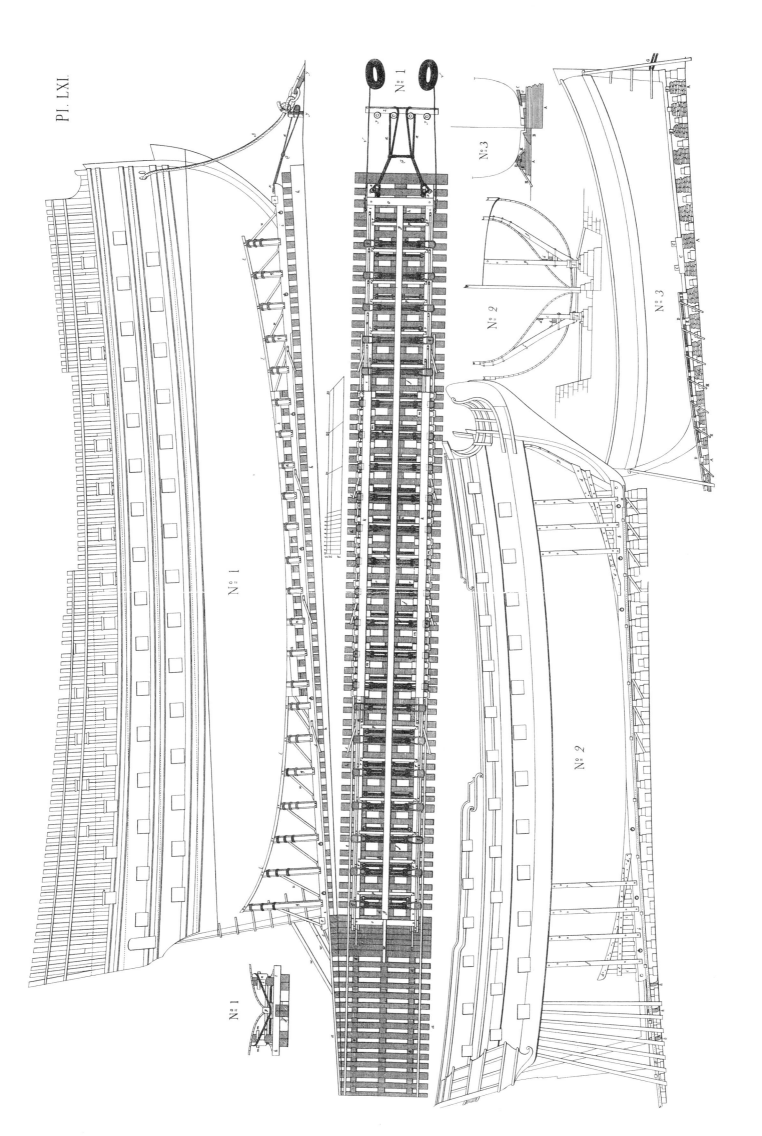

Pl. LXI.

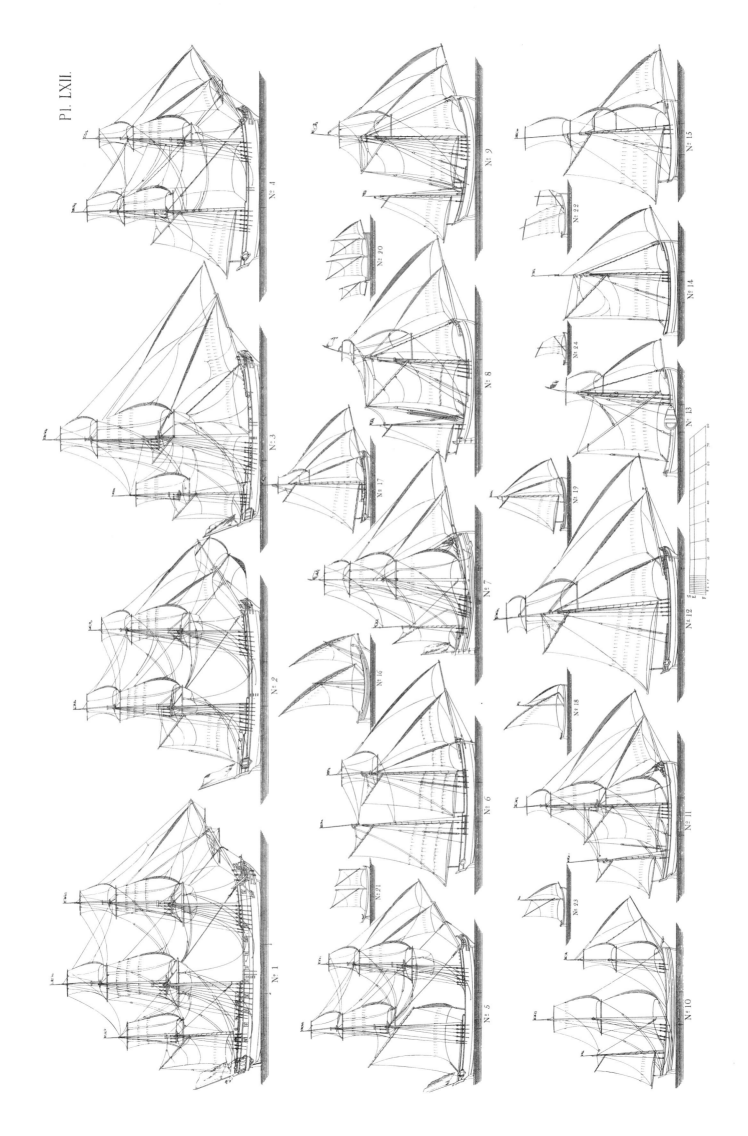

Pl. LXII.

N° 1

N° 2

N° 3

N° 4

N° 5

N° 6

N° 7

N° 8

N° 9

N° 10

N° 11

N° 12

N° 13

N° 14

N° 15

N° 16

N° 17

N° 18

N° 19

N° 20

N° 21

N° 22

N° 23

N° 24

The Author's Preface

If we were to take a view of the immense number of ships that have been built, since mankind first began to navigate upon the ocean, and note all the different steps, which have been taken in improving their construction, we should at first sight be inclined to believe, that the art of ship-building had, at length, been brought to the utmost perfection. An opinion that would receive additional force from a consideration of the few essential alterations, which have been introduced either in their form or rigging, during our own age.

Yet when we recollect the different kinds of ships and vessels, that are used in Europa, it will appear less surprising to us, if there should be good grounds for asserting that their very great variety, equally with other causes, have prevented ship-builders and riggers from discovering either the true figure and shape of ships, or the best mode of rigging them, either generally, or, for each species of vessel in particular.

In order to form a decisive opinion in both these points of view, on the degree of perfection to which ships in general have arrived, we will divide those of all nations into two classes; comprising in one, all small vessels, or those used in short voyages and narrow waters; in the other, all larger ships, or those employed in distant voyages, and calculated for going out to sea.

The first class consists of the vessels, that different natives make use of in their coasting trade, or in their commerce with neighbouring countries. As the climate, the extent and depth of the seas, the position of the countries with respect to the sea and to each other, also their productions, are different in different countries, the proportion and form of these vessels, as well as the mode of rigging them, must necessarily depend upon these circumstances. Thus a species of perfection may be found in the circumstance, that they are dissimilar in the same degree as their objects differ.

On the contrary, if we consider the ships comprehended in the second class, even though of different countries, we shall find that being built for the same purposes, they are similar in their essential parts. As to their proportions, we find that the breadth is between one-third and one-fourth of the length; that the least have usually greater breadth in proportion to their length than the largest; that the draught of water is something greater or less than the half breadth. The height out of the water has also limits, which depend on the particular destination of the ship. The accommodations, moreover, in these ships, among all nations have a great similarity; they differ only in matters of small importance, in which each follows the plan that appears most convenient.

With respect to form, we see that all ships have their greatest breadth a little before the middle; that they are leaner aft than forward; that those designed for ships of burthen are fuller in the bottom; that those built for sailing are leaner there; that the stem and stern-post have a rake; that they have a greater draught of water aft than forward, &c. With regard to the rigging, most vessels have three masts, others two, and some only one; which depends on their size. These masts with respect to the ships and the manner of rigging them, have nearly the same proportions and the same place. They are also generally rigged in the same manner, except that some may have more or less sail, according to the judgment of the owner. All ships have their center of gravity a little before the middle of their length, and the center of gravity of the sails always before the center of gravity of the ship.

In this manner all ships designed for navigating in the open sea are constructed; and as this mode of construction is the result of an infinite number of trials and experiments, and of alterations made in consequence thereof, it would be improper to infringe on limits so established.

But although ships are thus confined as to their proportions, within certain limits, still however they admit of such variations in their form, as to produce an infinite number of qualities more or less good, or more or less bad.

There are ships possessing all the qualities, which we can reasonably wish for, and there are others, which, although within the abovementioned limits, have nevertheless a great many faults.

In the construction of ships, people usually make attempts at different times to improve the form, each person according to his own experience; thus after the construction of one ship, which has been tried and found to possess such or such a bad quality, it seems possible to remedy this defect in another. But it often (not to say generally) happens, that the new ship possesses some fault equally as great, and frequently even that the former defect, instead of being removed, is increased. And we are unable to determine, whether this fault proceeds from the fault of the ship, or from other unknown circumstances.

It thus appears, that the construction of a ship with more or less good qualities, is a matter of chance and not of previous design, and it hence follows, that as long as we are without a good theory on shipbuilding, and have nothing to trust to beyond bare experiments and trials, this art cannot be expected to acquire any greater perfection, than it possesses at present.

It becomes a matter of importance then, to discover what may bring this knowledge to greater perfection. Seeing that ships, the proportions of which lie within the same limits, nay, which have the same form, differ greatly from each other in respect to their qualities, and even that with a small alteration in the form, a ship acquires a quality immediately opposite to the one we wish to give it, we must conclude that this arises from certain physical causes; and that the art of constructing ships cannot be carried to greater perfection, till a theory has been discovered, which elucidates these causes.

In every art or science there exists a hidden theory, which is the more or less difficult to be found out, as the art or science depends more or less on physical causes.

Into the theory of a common oar, even Archimedes made researches, and many others after him; notwithstanding which, this theory is not yet fully explained. If such difficulties occur in this investigation, how great must those be which attend the theory of ship-building, where so many other circumstances are combined!

It is true, that the oar is made use of to great advantage in rowing, the cannon in firing; an infinite number of machines are in like manner used, without considering it absolutely necessary to investigate to the bottom their theory. We see how little these machines can be advanced towards perfection by its assistance. The question may be perhaps concerning some inches more or less in the length of the oar, concerning a twentieth part less matter for a cannon of the same force; so that the theory for these objects is not so necessary as for ships.

For ships, we have to fear an infinity of bad qualities of the greatest consequence, which we are never sure of being able to remove, without understanding the theory.

At the same time the construction of ships and their equipment, are attended with too great expense, not to endeavour beforehand to insure their good qualities and their suitableness for what they are intended for. The theory then which elucidates the causes of these different qualities, which determines whether the defects of a ship proceed from its form, or from other causes, is truly important; but as the theory is unlimited, practice must determine its limits. We may consequently farther conclude, that the art of ship-building can never be carried to the last degree of perfection, nor all possible good qualities be given to ships, before we at the same time possess in the most perfect degree possible, a knowledge both of the theory and practice.

To possess this theory in all its extent seems to exceed the force of the human understanding. We are obliged therefore to content ourselves with a part of this vast science; that is, with knowing sufficient of it to give to ships the principal good qualities, which I conceive to be:

1. That a ship with a certain draught of water, should be able to contain and carry a determinate lading.

2. That it should have a sufficient and also determinate stability.

3. That it should be easy at sea, or its rolling and pitching not too quick.

4. That it should sail well before the wind, and close to the wind, and work well to windward.

5. That it should not be too ardent, and yet come easily about.

Of these qualities one part is at variance with another; it is necessary therefore to try so to unite theory and practice, that no more is lost in one object than is necessary in order to secure another, so that the sum of both may be a maximum.

This is the subject of this short treatise. Whether I have succeeded or not, will be seen by the reader. There will be found in it some things both in theory and practice, which have not hitherto been treated of, and which may be worthy of the attention of persons who are desirous of applying themselves to this science; it will be seen moreover, that the principles laid down admit of demonstration, although they are of the most difficult nature.

Still however it must be confessed, that this science has one great difficulty, in which it probably differs from all others; namely, that even after following the theory with the greatest exactness, and executing the work, according to its rules, with the greatest care, the constructor may notwithstanding suffer in point of professional reputation. For although a ship may have been built in conformity with all the rules which both theory and practice prescribe, its yards have got their true proportions, and the masts their true place and position; so that there appears to be the greatest certainty of its possessing all the best qualities; it may nevertheless happen, that such a vessel will answer very ill for the following reasons:

1. Although the rigging of the ship (when the masts and yards are put in their place, and are in due proportion) is not a matter of such great difficulty, but that every seaman knows how to give the proper proportions, it happens, notwithstanding, that too stout cordage and too large pullies are frequently used, which renders the weights aloft too considerable. It may happen also that the sails are badly cut, on which account the ship may lose the advantage of sailing well close to the wind, of coming about, &c. whence great inconveniences may result, with which the form of the ship has nothing to do.

2. The ship is liable also to become ungovernable, to lose its good qualities in every way by the bad disposition of the stowage. If the lading be too low, the moment of stability will become too great, which will occasion violent

rolling. On the contrary, if the weight of the lading be too much raised, the ship will not carry sail well when the wind blows fresh; neither will it be able to work off a lee shore; if the lading be too heavy towards the extremities, it will produce heavy sending and pitching, whence the ship may become the worst possible sailer, with other inconveniences which are not the fault of the ship itself.

3. The good performance of a ship depends also on the manner in which it is worked; for if the sails be not well set, with respect to the direction of the wind and the course, it will lose in point of sailing; it will become slack so as to miss stays, which often places a ship in a critical situation. The person who works the ship is also charged with an attention to the draught of water; and to the manner of setting up the shrouds and stays, upon which the qualities of the ship greatly depend. Furthermore, to work the ship well is of greater consequence in a privateer, than in a merchant ship. One who understands the management of his ship, knows how to give it all the good qualities it is capable of; he knows how to employ those qualities to his advantage, and when he is engaged with an enemy, he thereby makes himself master of the attack; but he who blunders in the working of his ship, may thereby not only be reduced to the necessity of acting solely on the defensive, but seldom if ever escapes falling an easy prey to the enemy, although his ship is ever so carefully and well built.

Thus an owner may suffer considerable losses, in a thousand ways, less through the defects of his ship, than the ignorance of the commander.

It is even frequently observed, that a ship exhibits the best qualities, during one cruise, and the very worst during another.

Lastly, it is evident from all that has been said, that a ship of the best form, will not shew its good qualities, except it is at the same time well rigged, well stowed, and well worked by those who command it.

When a ship is at rest, the pressure of the water upon each of its extremities is the same; but as soon as it is impelled by any force, the pressure is increased at the end opposite to the impulse, and is diminished at that end where it acts: this we shall explain hereafter.

If a plane is moved in the water, the resistance is the most forcible, when the direction of motion is perpendicular to the plane, and becomes less if the plane assumes a position oblique to the line of motion.

Thus bodies of different forms and convexities, with equal bases, experience different resistances.

It is by no means difficult to express the resistance, which one body meets with in striking another: but it is not equally easy to express the effect which a medium produces on bodies, which are moved therein. The effect of the impact of bodies on each other is subject to known mechanical laws, but that of mediums upon bodies depends on physical causes, with which we are unacquainted.

To surmount this difficulty, fluids have been supposed to consist of globular particles, infinitely small, which follow each other very closely, and strike the body in succession; as for example:

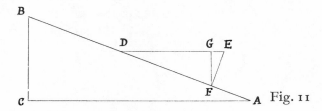

Fig. 11

Let *ABC* (Fig. 11) be a right-angled triangle, suppose the fluid, or a particle of the fluid, to strike the side *AB* of this triangle in a direction parallel to *AC*, from *A* to *C*, with the velocity *ED*.

If *ED* denote the perpendicular resistance against the base *BC*, it may be resolved into two others, *EF* perpendicular and *FD* parallel to *AD*; as the effect in the direction *FD* is nothing, inasmuch as the fluid glides along *AB*, therefore *EF* alone acts on the triangle, and in a direction perpendicular to *AB*; in like manner this force may be resolved into two others, *GF* perpendicular and *EG* parallel to *AC*; *GF* is the lateral force, which impels the triangle from *B* to *C*, but *EG* denotes the direct force, which acts on the side *AB*, and consequently the resistance: thus the absolute or perpendicular resistance at the point *D* is to the relative resistance as *ED* to *EG*; but $DE:EG::DE^2:EF^2$; and since the number of particles, which can strike the side *AB* in the direction *ED* are in proportion to *BC*, and from similar triangles *DEF*, *ABC* we have $DE:EF::AB:BC$, the direct resistance against the whole triangle is as $\frac{BC^2}{AB^2} \times BC.$

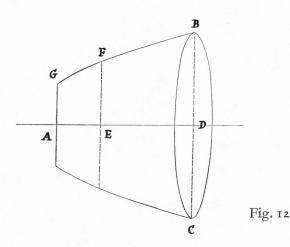

Fig. 12

Upon this principle the known curve *GFB* (Fig. 12) of least resistance has been investigated, which is of such a nature, that by revolving round its axis *AD* it generates a solid *AGBD*, which experiences less resistance from the water than any body whatever of the same length *AD* and the same base *BC*. As this problem is treated on by several authors, I shall here only give the construction of the curve.

If $AE = x$, $EF = y$, the equation will be $y\dot{y}^3\dot{x} = a \times (\dot{x}^2 = \dot{y}^2)^2$ (see Simpson's Fluxions, Art. 413.).

The angle AGF has been found to be a right angle and a half, or $135°$. Let $v = \dfrac{\dot{x}}{\dot{y}}$; then $\dot{x} = v \times \dot{y}$, and $\dot{x}^2 = v^2 \times \dot{y}^2$.

Substituting the value of $\dot{x}^2$ in the equation, we have $vy\dot{y}^4 = a \times (v^2\dot{y}^2 + \dot{y}^2)^2$, or $vy = a \times (v^4 + 2\,v^2 + 1)$; hence $y = a \times \left(v^3 + 2\,v + \dfrac{1}{v}\right)$ and $\dot{y} = a \times \left(3\,v^2\dot{v} + 2\,\dot{v} - \dfrac{\dot{v}}{v^2}\right)$ and therefore $\dot{x} = a \times \left(3\,v^3\dot{v} + 2v\dot{v} - \dfrac{\dot{v}}{v}\right)$ of which the fluent or $x = a \times \left(\dfrac{3}{4}v^4 + v^2 - \log. v\right) + C$. When $v = 1$, then $x = 0$ by the above-mentioned property, whence $\dfrac{7}{4}a + C = 0$, and $C = -\dfrac{7}{4}a$; hence $x = a \times \left(\dfrac{3}{4}v^4 + v^2 - \dfrac{7}{4} - \log. v\right)$. Supposing $a = 1$, the least ordinate AG will be equal to 4.

If, beginning with 1, we give successive values to v, and substitute them in the equation of x and y, we shall have the following values of x and y.

$v = 1,0$	$x = 0$ $y = 4$	$v = 1,06$	$x = 0,262$ $y = 4,254$	$v = 1,1$	$x = 0,453$ $y = 4,440$
$v = 1,2$	$x = 1,053$ $y = 4,961$	$v = 1,3$	$x = 1,820$ $y = 5,566$	$v = 1,4$	$x = 2,655$ $y = 6,258$
$v = 1,5$	$x = 3,892$ $y = 7,042$	$v = 1,6$	$x = 5,255$ $y = 7,921$	$v = 1,7$	$x = 6,873$ $y = 8,901$
$v = 1,8$	$x = 8,775$ $y = 9,987$	$v = 2,0$	$x = 13,557$ $y = 12,500$	$v = 2,2$	$x = 19,900$ $y = 15,502$

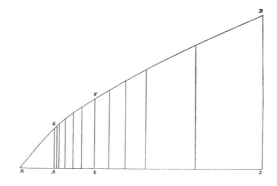

Fig. 13

Let $AE = x$, $EF = y$ (Fig. 13); then from A the values of x are set off on AD, and on the corresponding ordinates AG, EF, &c. the values of y, we shall have the line GFB, which as we have said, by revolving round its axis AD, will generate a solid, which will experience less resistance than any other body of the same length AD, and of the same base BD. If this solid be terminated by a cone AHG whose base $= AG$, the resistance by that means will be considerably diminished.

We shall see by the following Articles the quantity of resistance, which a body like this meets with from the fluid.

When a body is at rest in the water, it receives a pressure at every point of the part immersed, which is perpendicular to its surface, and its force proportional to the depth of the part pressed.

This is a fact derived from experience, which it is necessary not to lose sight of: but before we go farther into the investigation of the expression for the resistance, which a body meets with when impelled through a fluid, it is necessary to notice the circumstances which occur, when a ship sails forward, or when a ship by means of any force whatever is drawn through the water.

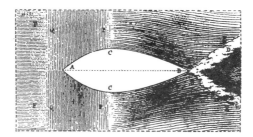

Fig. 14

When a ship *ABC* (Fig. 14) is put in motion in still water with any velocity, it always happens that the water upon the extremity *A* before the greatest breadth *C*, rises against this part above the surface *F*. This elevation is perceptible to some distance before the ship in the direction of its course; it also extends laterally towards *PQ*; but past the greatest breadth *C*, the water falls again, so that between *C* and *B* it is below its proper level, until it meets in *D* the part of the fluid, which constantly follows the ship with the same velocity as the ship has itself, in order to fill up the void space, which it would leave behind. But as the water, which glides along the side of the ship, has already filled this space, there is a collision of this fluid in *EE*, which produces what is called eddy water. This is a thing remarked more in small vessels, which draw little water; but in great vessels, the elevation of the water afore is not perceptible till they have attained a velocity of 4 or 5 feet in a second. This water, which is before the greatest breadth, is driven forward with the ship, and so moves in the same direction; and as it is higher afore the greatest breadth than abaft, it flows down a declivity, so as to acquire a velocity in a direction contrary to that of the ship; and the greater velocity the ship has, the greater is this declivity.

All this is sufficiently observable, when a ship is navigated in a sea little agitated, where there are no waves: but when a ship sails or is drawn along a channel, where there is not more than three or four times the breadth of the ship between it and the side of the channel, this effect is much more perceptible, however small may be the velocity.

There necessarily results from what we have just observed; first, that the resistance a ship sailing with a given velocity meets with, is increased on account of the water's rising before the greatest breadth, and because the ship has to propel a more elevated body of water before it, than at the commencement of its motion; although this column thus elevated and driven a-head, by acting on the water in the direction of its motion, before the body of the ship gets to the same point, in some degree diminishes the resistance. Secondly, that the resistance is farther increased, because the water is lower behind the greatest breadth, and because this water has, moreover, lost in regard to its pressure against the after part of the ship, a force which depends on the velocity of the ship, and also on that with which the fluid flows along the after parts of the ship, in running from the greatest breadth of the ship to the stern-post.

After the observations and remarks which have been made, let us form an equation, which expresses the resistance that a body meets with when impelled through the water.

A difficulty occurs however, which arises from the circumstance of its being necessary to compare the pressure of the water with the effect arising from the velocity of the body, two forces, which are of very different kinds. But since we may neglect in the expression the perpendicular pressure of the water against the surface of the ship when at rest (the effect being the same, whatever be the extremity of the body that moves forward), we may observe that the force in question expresses only the effect of the inequality of the pressure on the two extremities of the ship during the motion, or the resistance, which is thereby occasioned, and which depends as to its amount on the velocity of the ship.

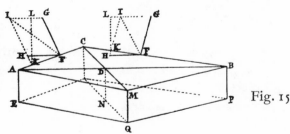

Fig. 15

Let *ACBQ* (Fig. 15) be formed of two wedges joined together at their base *CQ*; let the pressure of the water, perpendicular to the surface in every point, be denoted by *FG*, *FG*.

Suppose this body to be moved with the velocity *FH* in a direction parallel to the middle line *AB*, from *B* to *A*; complete in the usual manner the parallelogram *FGIH*, and draw the diagonal *IF*. Then we have the resultant of this velocity with the pressure of the water in the direction *IF*. If from the point *K*, where the line *IH* meets the line *AC* or *CB*, we draw the line *KL* perpendicular to *GI*, *IL* will be the resistance, which the body experiences in the direction *BA*, and *LI* is a force on the hinder part of the body *CB*, which impels it forward in the direction in which it moves.

Let *CM* be perpendicular to *AB*; *CD* = *DM*, and *DN* be perpendicular to the surface *ACBM*. Let *FG* = *m*, *FH* = *n*; the area of the plane *CE* = *A*, the area of the plane *CP* = *B*, and lastly the area of the plane *CN* = *C*.

From the similar triangles *ACD*, *FHK*, *KIL*, we have $KH = \dfrac{DC}{AC} \times n$, and hence $IK = \dfrac{DC}{AC} \times n + m$, and also $IL = \dfrac{DC}{AC} \times \left(m + \dfrac{DC}{AC} \times n\right)$. *IL* represents the resistance at the point *F*, which is produced by the forces *FG* (*m*),

HF (n). But the number of pressures FG is to the number of pressures FH, as the area A is to the area C; conse-quently $A \times \dfrac{DC}{AC} \times m + C \times \dfrac{DC^2}{AC^2} \times n$ represents the effect of the water on the forepart. In the same manner we get

$B \times \dfrac{DC}{BC} \times m - C \times \dfrac{DC^2}{BC^2} \times n$ for the effect of the water on the aft part.

Subtracting this last expression from the first, the resistance against this body moved in the direction AB, will be

expressed by $A \times \dfrac{DC}{AC} \times m + C \times \dfrac{DC^2}{AC^2} \times n - B \times \dfrac{DC}{BC} \times m + C \times \dfrac{DC^2}{BC^2} \times n$, and as $A \times \dfrac{DC}{AC} \times m = B \times \dfrac{DC}{BC} \times m$,

the expression for the resistance is reduced to $C \times \dfrac{DC^2}{AC^2} \times n + C \times \dfrac{DC^2}{BC^2} \times n$; whence we see, so long as the velocity

is not sufficient to produce an elevation of the water afore, and a depression abaft the greatest breadth, so as to increase the fore resistance and diminish that aft, that the body will experience the same resistance, whether the sharp or obtuse extremity moves forward; and yet that the resistance will be the least when the two extremities are equal, or what is the same thing, when the greatest breadth CM is in the middle.

But if we suppose that the water runs a-head of the ship before its greatest breadth with a velocity v, and that it has acquired a velocity w in a direction opposite to that of the body abaft this greatest breadth, then the velocity forward $= n - v$, and aft $= n + w$; and as the resistance is in proportion to the squares of the velocities, it will be

expressed definitively by $C' \times \dfrac{DC^2}{AC^2} \times (n - v)^2 + C \times \dfrac{DC^2}{BC^2} \times (n + w)^2$, where we suppose C' to be greater than C,

inasmuch as the water before the greatest breadth is more elevated than behind it.

Hence it is seen, whatever proportion there is between n, v, and w, the body meets with less resistance, when the obtuse end is forward, than when the acute end is forward; and that it depends on the quantities $n - v$, and $n + w$, how far the main breadth should be before the middle point, so that the resistance may be less, than if its situation were anywhere else.

We see also that the greater v and w are with respect to n, the more the greatest breadth should be carried before the middle to render the resistance least.

It never can happen that $v = n$, for in this case, the water, would run forward with the same velocity as the ship, which is not possible. v is very small with respect to n, when the velocity is little; so that when n is very small $v = $ o. It is the same also in respect to the water abaft the greatest breadth; when the velocity is small and the body has its greatest breadth very far aft, the water follows the body to fill up the void space which it leaves; from which cause a part of the water follows the same direction as the body, so that the velocity of the body in relation to the water is $n - w$, whence it follows that the expression for the resistance ought to have this form

$$C' \times \dfrac{DC^2}{AC^2} \times (n - v)^2 + C \times \dfrac{DC^2}{BC^2} \times (n \pm w)^2.$$

If this expression for the resistance be not exact, at least what results from it is confirmed by the following experi-ments.

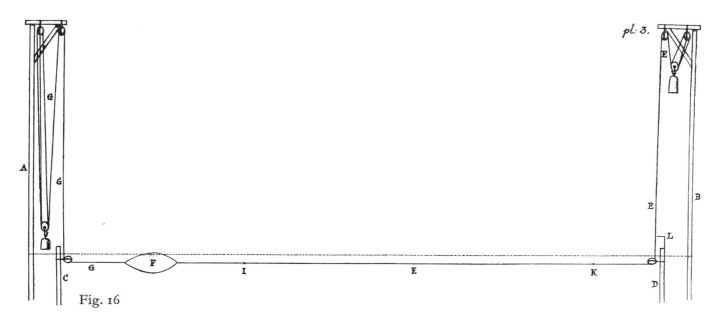

Fig. 16

In a large and deep pond (Fig. 16) were placed a hundred feet from each other two poles A, B, and two piles C, D, to which were fitted two copper pullies, and through these were reeved ropes to support the weights; the whole as is represented in the figure. The lines E and G were attached to the body used in the experiment. On the line E a weight was placed, to give motion to the body in the water, and on the other line G there was also a weight, but less than the first, to keep the body in a straight line from which it would have deviated without it; to the line E were tied two small pieces of red cloth I, K, at the distance of 74 feet from each other. To measure the time a stopwatch shewing seconds was used. When the mark arrived at L the stop-watch was let go, and when the mark I was come to the same point, the watch was stopped. It then shewed the number of seconds which the body F took up to pass over the space of 74 feet. The bodies, on which the experiments were made, were of wood, and were 28 inches in length; the transverse sections under the water were circular. Their diameters at the greatest breadth were 2/7 of the length, or 8 inches; the water-lines were either straight or conic parabolas, and the vertex of the parabolic line was at the greatest breadth. As these bodies were lighter than water, lead was run in, until their specific gravity was nearly equal to that of sea water, so that they only just floated, having their axes parallel to the surface of the water. The weight on the line E to put the body in motion, was varied according as it was required to increase or diminish the velocity; but the retarding weight was always the same. The bodies N°. 1, 2, and 3 had the same weight, but the others were lighter in proportion as the solidity of a cone is less than that of a paraboloid.

Weight of the bodies		N°. 1 27 pounds	N°. 2 27 pounds		N°. 3 27 pounds		N°. 4 22 pounds		N°. 5 19 3/4 pounds		N°. 6 16 3/4 pounds		N°. 7 12 pounds	
Form of the bodies		A　　A	B	C	D	E	F	G	H	I	O	P	R	P
Moving weights	Retarding weights	Time the bodies have been describing the space of 74 feet, in seconds												
		Seconds A	Seconds B	C	D	E	F	G	H	I	O	P	R	P
3/4 the weight of the body	1/2 the weight of the body	25 1/2	26 1/4	24 3/4	27 3/4	26 1/2	25 3/4	25 1/2	27 1/4	24 1/4	30	29 3/4	45	29 1/2
The weight of the body	1/2 the weight of the body	14	14	14 1/2	14 1/2	16 1/2	13 3/4	13 3/4	15	16	24 1/2	24 1/4	38	24
1 1/2 weight of the body	1/2 the weight of the body	11	10 1/2	11 1/2	10 1/2	13 1/2	11	11	10 1/4	11 1/2	12 1/2	17 1/2	30 3/4	19 1/4
37 pounds in all	12 lb. and 1/3 in all	12 1/2	lost		11	14	10 3/4	11	10	11 1/4	12	16	—	—

The bodies N°. 1. has its greatest breadth at the middle, and its two extremities formed by parabolic lines.

        N°. 2. has its greatest breadth at 2/7 of its length from the point B; the two extremities are also parabolic.

        N°. 3. has its greatest breadth 1/7 of the length from the point D; the two extremities still parabolic.

        N°. 4. has its greatest breadth at the middle; the extremity F parabolic, the other G conic.

        N°. 5. has its greatest breadth 2/7 of the length from the point H; the extremity H parabolic, the other I conic.

        N°. 6. has its greatest breadth 2/7 of the length from O; the two extremities conic.

        N°. 7. wholly conic, having the greatest breadth equal to that of the other bodies, and its length twice and an half the breadth.

To understand these experiments take N°. 2, where the moving weight is equal to that of the body, and the retarding weight is half of it. With the extremity B first, the body passes over 74 feet in 14 seconds; if on the contrary the extremity C be first, the body is 14 1/2 seconds in passing over the same space.

Each of these experiments was repeated six times, and a mean taken of the results, which for the most part were nearly equal; and where there was any difference, it did not exceed half a second. We do not find in the velocities, the proportions we are led to expect from a consideration of the weights; which arises from a motion produced at the surface of the water by a division of the fluid too near the surface. The number of pullies over which the line passes, renders the experiments less exact on account of friction. But as the friction is equal for all the experiments, the variation of velocity ought to be of the same kind.

The inferences which we may draw from all this are; first, that when the motion is slow, the body has greater velocity when the sharp end is forward than when the full; secondly, that when the velocity is increased to a certain degree, the body passes over the same distance in equal times, with either extremity forward; thirdly, that when the velocity becomes still greater, the body is less time in passing over the same distance, when the obtuse end is forward. Thus it is the velocity of the body which should determine the place of the greatest breadth, to render the resistance least.

M. Camus, in his Treatise on Moving Forces, speaks of experiments which he made to determine this point. We find likewise (Murray's Treatise on Ship-building) some experiments, which agree with the above sufficiently well; differing however from them in this, that whether the velocity is great or little, the body always experiences less resistance when the fullest end is forward, a circumstance which arises from the experiments having been made in a canal formed on purpose, in proportion to the breadth of which that of the body was considerable; so that the water could not pass it without rising before, and consequently being lower behind. This water must therefore have had a current on each side of the body, so that however slowly the body was moved in the canal, the effect of the water was the same, as when in the above experiments it was moved with the greatest velocity.

These experiments are agrerable to the expression for the resistance which was given in the previous articles. The only question is to find the value of v and w relatively to n, and to see when we ought to employ the signs $+$ and $-$ in $n \pm w$. We know from what was previously said that the sign $-$ in $n \pm w$ is not to be used in the expression for the resistance, except when the velocity and the form behind the greatest breadth are such, that the water, which acts on the after part, moves in the same direction as the ship.

On the dimensions of ships

As we cannot conclude any thing from the last Articles concerning the proportions, which ought to take place between the length, breadth, and depth of the ship, and since its qualities depend greatly upon these proportions, it is necessary to enumerate those qualities, which are essential to a merchant ship; in order thence to determine the proportions most advantageous, and most likely to produce such or such qualities, which may be required.

A merchant ship ought:

1. To be able to carry a great lading in proportion to its size.
2. To sail well by the wind, in order to beat easily off a coast where it may be embayed, and also to come about well in a hollow sea.
3. To work with a crew small in number in proportion to its cargo.
4. To be able to sail with a small quantity of ballast.

To procure these advantages to a ship, it appears:

1. That to take a great lading with respect to its size, it ought to have great breadth and depth, in proportion to its length, and to be full in the bottom. Such a ship would also work with a small number of hands in proportion to its cargo. But it would neither sail well nor beat to wind-ward.
2. That to give the property of sailing and beating to windward, to the end that it might beat off a lee shore, as well as come about well in a hollow sea, the ship must necessarily have a considerable moment of stability in proportion to the plane of resistance, that it may be able to carry a press of sail, notwithstanding a strong wind; with this view is is necessary to give to the ship in question, great breadth in proportion to its length; to fill it much towards the

load water-line, curtailing it in the bottom. Such a ship would require a numerous crew because of the largeness of the sails, and the weight of its anchors.

3. That if it be required to navigate a ship with few men, in proportion to the lading, it should have a small surface of sails, and anchors of small weight. For this purpose it should have little breadth in proportion to its length.

It would also be enabled to carry a great lading, in proportion to its equipment of men, by giving it great fulness in its bottom; but such a ship would sail badly close to the wind, and would come about with difficulty in a hollow sea.

4. That to enable a ship to sail with a small quantity of ballast, it is necessary to fill the body between wind and water, when it has the ballast in; it should be large and little elevated above the water. A ship of this kind would carry a sufficient lading in proportion to its size, but it would ply badly when laden, especially if it were a large ship; without giving it a considerable quantity of sail, which would render it necessary to have a great number of men.

By this it is again proved, that we can conclude nothing concerning the length, breadth, and depth of ships, since different qualities require conditions diametrically opposite to each other. We may succeed in uniting two of these advantages by a certain form and by certain proportions given to ships, but it is impossible to combine all four in an eminent degree. It is not possible to gain on one side without losing on another.

Wherefore, for a merchant ship, it is necessary to combine these qualities, so that it may have the most possible of each. That is to say, that the expression representing the velocity and quantity of lading divided by the number of the crew and quantity of ballast, may be a *maximum*.

Again, however, as certain commercial speculations require one quality in preference to another; the nature of this commerce; the latitudes in which it is necessary to navigate; the ports for anchorage; all these must be considered in determining which of these qualities ought to prevail, without altering in any respect the size of the ship.

We must again observe that the qualities of similar ships vary in a different proportion from what a consideration of their size would give.

If the breadth be represented by the variable quantity B, the burden of the ship will vary in the proportion of B^3; the velocity of sailing $\dfrac{B^{1/2} \times L^{4/3}}{D^{3/2}}$ will vary as $B^{1/3}$, and the number of the crew, which is proportional to the area of the sails $B^2 L^{2/3}$, will vary in the proportion of $B^{8/3}$. So that, supposing two ships to be similar, the one of 320 lasts, and the other an eighth of this capacity or 40 lasts, whilst the larger will sail ten knots, the small one will only sail eight; and if the great one sail with a crew of twenty-four men, the small one will require four. According to the capacities of the two ships, it ought to be navigable by three men. Hence we see, that *in making small ships similar to large ones, the former will sail worse, and will require a more numerous crew in proportion to their capacities than the large ones.*

We have seen above, that we may obtain for a small ship a property of sailing equal to that of a large one, by increasing its moment of stability, and diminishing the plane of resistance; but as then it would have a greater quantity of sails, it would be necessary to increase the number of the crew.

It is possible to render a small ship navigable by a crew proportionate to its capacity, but it cannot be done without diminishing the quantity of canvass, and then the vessel will sail worse. One may remedy this fault to a certain point, by giving it less breadth; but we have seen that this would not be without inconvenience; so that upon the whole, we find that it is necessary to prefer, in small ships, the property of sailing well, to having it in our power to economise in the number of the crew.

The velocity being in proportion to $\dfrac{B^{1/2} L^{4/3}}{D^{3/2}}$, it increases as the depth decreases, supposing at the same time the length and breadth to increase. The object is attained more easily by adding to the length, but for the greatest safety of the navigation, in order that the ship overtaken by a squall may come to the wind, and that it may come about easily in a heavy sea, it is more convenient to increase its breadth, whence the metacenter will be more elevated; the sails may then have a greater surface; but once again, the ship would require a more numerous crew.

We see then, that *great and small ships cannot, with the same form, sail with the same security,* and that we cannot avoid the inconvenience of being obliged to have a more numerous crew in proportion in small ships; as in the place of four men, six, &c.

So that small ships cannot have the same advantages as large ones, when it is required to employ them in the same trade.

As small ships lose in the quality of sailing, by being of a form similar to that of large ones, also large ones would gain in this respect by being shaped like small ones; we may thence conclude that it is proper to give to large ships the same form which small ones have; since thereby they would gain in the quality of sailing. But for merchant ships, where it is so much the more necessary to give great capacities in the water, as they are the more large, and as they seldom want a superior quality of sailing, provided they are sufficiently stiff upon a wind not to be embayed on a lee shore; considering besides, that these ships would lose the advantage of sailing with a small crew, and moreover, that a large ship costs more in its construction in proportion than a small one: for this kind of ships, I say, it is necessary to try to combine qualities the most advantageous to the interest of the owner.

All these inquiries do not bring us to the determination of the proportion to be given between the length, breadth, and depth of the ships, and we see that theory alone is not sufficient for this purpose: it becomes necessary therefore to introduce practice, and to see by several trials and various experiments, in what manner different ships answer in different cases. Then we may, by means of the above expressions, give to large or small ships the qualities which we wish, and carry them to a certain degree with relation to those of a known ship.

Species of ship	Burthen in lasts reduced into cubic feet, reckoning 91 cubic feet for each last	Displacement in cubic feet to the outside of the timbers	Length from the perpendicular at the stem to that at the sternpost	Greatest breadth to the outside of the timbers	Distances of the load water-line from the upper edge of the rabbet of the keel, at the frame $\oplus$	Area of the midship section	Depth of the keel measured from the upper edge of the rabbet	Difference of draught of water
	P	D	x	z	h	$\oplus$	k	d
Frigates	$D^{17/18}$	$P^{18/17}$	$\overline{56 D^{1/3}}$	$\dfrac{x^{4/5}}{1,383}$	$\dfrac{x}{8,1}$	$\dfrac{1,705\, D}{x^{1+1/40}}$	$\dfrac{x^{2/5}}{4,64}$	$\dfrac{x^{3/4}}{23,3}$
Heckboats or Pinks	$D^{19/20}$	$P^{20/19}$	$\overline{54 D^{1/3}}$	$\dfrac{x^{4/5}}{1,429}$	$\dfrac{x^{1-1/60}}{7,547}$	$\dfrac{1,729\, D}{x^{1+1/27}}$	$\dfrac{x^{3/7}}{5,66}$	$\dfrac{x^{2/3}}{17,5}$
Cats or Barks	$D^{21/22}$	$P^{22/21}$	$\overline{52 D^{1/3}}$	$\dfrac{x^{4/5}}{1,476}$	$\dfrac{x^{1-1/30}}{7,032}$	$\dfrac{1,76\, D}{x^{1+1/20}}$	$\dfrac{x^{1/2}}{8,4}$	$\dfrac{x^{2/3}}{18,8}$
Flat-bottomed Vessels, or Vessels with a small draught of water	$1,07\, D^{21/22}$	$\dfrac{P^{22/21}}{1,07}$	$\overline{63 D^{1/3}}$	$\dfrac{x^{4/5}}{1,6}$	$\dfrac{x^{1-1/10}}{6,436}$	$\dfrac{2,1\, D}{x^{1+1/10}}$	$\dfrac{x^{1/2}}{9,8}$	$\dfrac{x^{2/3}}{24}$

Species of ship	Area of the load water-line	Quantity by which the center of gravity of the displacement is below the load water-line	$\int_{\frac{2}{3}} \times \dfrac{y^3 \dot{x}}{D}$	Fraction of the distance between the center of gravity of displacement and the load water-line, which the center of gravity of the ship and lading is below the water	Distance of the metacenter from the center of gravity of the ship and lading	Moment of stability
	W	V	S		L	M
Frigates	$\dfrac{z\, x^{1+1/30}}{1,49}$	$\dfrac{x^{7/6}}{48}$	$\dfrac{x^{1/2}}{1,289}$	$\dfrac{1}{4}$	$\dfrac{49,65\, x^{1/2} - x^{7/6}}{64}$	$\dfrac{x^3}{56} \times \dfrac{49,65\, x^{1/2} - x^{7/6}}{64}$
Heckboats or Pinks	$\dfrac{z\, x^{1+1/24}}{1,5}$	$\dfrac{x^{139/120}}{45,54}$	$\dfrac{x^{21/40}}{1,651}$	$\dfrac{2}{7}$	$\dfrac{38,8\, x^{21/40} - x^{139/120}}{64}$	$\dfrac{x^3}{54} \times \dfrac{38,8\, x^{21/40} - x^{139/120}}{64}$
Cats or Barks	$\dfrac{z\, x^{1+1/20}}{1,5}$	$\dfrac{x^{23/20}}{43,2}$	$\dfrac{x^{11/20}}{2,147}$	$\dfrac{1}{3}$	$\dfrac{30\, x^{11/20} - x^{23/20}}{64}$	$\dfrac{x^3}{52} \times \dfrac{30\, x^{11/20} - x^{23/20}}{64}$
Flat-bottomed Vessels, or Vessels with a small draught of water	$\dfrac{z\, x^{1+1/30}}{1,4}$	$\dfrac{x}{26}$	$\dfrac{x^{1/2}}{1,341}$	$\dfrac{1}{5}$	$\dfrac{24,23\, x^{1/2} - x}{32,5}$	$\dfrac{x^3}{63} \times \dfrac{24,23\, x^{1/2} - x}{32,5}$

The preceding table N°. 1, according to which we may regulate all the proportions of merchant ships from the largest, as those engaged in the India trade, to the smallest, is founded on experience, and may serve as a guide in preparing the draught of a ship of any required tonnage.

But as it is not possible to form a ship, which combines in a certain degree all the qualities which may be wished, for this reason we have given in the table four species of ships.

In the construction of the first kind, under the denomination of *frigates*, it is to be considered, that they are to navigate in seas where hostilities are to be apprehended; which renders it necessary that they should carry a certain quantity of artillery, and at the same time sail well; and since the service of artillery requires a certain number of men, we may give to the ship a greater quantity of sail. With cannon, a ship has great weight above the water; besides it has to carry a greater quantity of sail; to have sufficient stability, it ought therefore to have its metacenter of a proper height above the load water-line. On which account it should have great length and breadth in proportion to the capacity of the hull.

The third kind, under the denomination of *barks* or *cats*, have few or no guns; they are built solely for trade; and their object is to carry the greatest possible lading, and sail with the smallest possible number of men. It is necessary that they possess, as far as it is practicable, the qualities which have been the subject of the above Articles.

The second species, under the denominations of *heckboats or pinks*, is that of vessels, which in regard to qualities, preserve a mean between the first and the third.

The fourth species, under the denomination of *flat-bottomed vessels*, have the same qualities with the third; but not having so great a draught of water when laden they want less ballast.

It will be more plainly seen by the tables and plans contained in my book of plates, what difference there is between these three species of ships.

Logarithms

$$P = 18200 = 4,2600714$$
$$P^{22/21} = D = 4,4676938 = 29350$$
$$52 = 1,7160033$$
$$3)\ 6,1836971$$
$$x = 2,0612323 = 115,14$$
$$4$$
$$5)\ 8,2449292$$
$$x^{4/5} = 1,6489858$$
$$1,476 = 0,1690864$$
$$z = 1,4798994 = 30,19$$
$$x = 2,0612323$$
$$0,0687077$$
$$x^{1 - 1/30} = 1,9925246$$
$$7,032 = 0,8470789$$
$$h = 1,1454457 = 13,978$$
$$x = 2,0612323$$
$$0,1030616$$
$$x^{1 + 1/20} = 2,1642939$$
$$1,76 = 0,2455127$$
$$D = 4,4676938$$
$$4,7132065$$
$$x^{1 + 1/20} = 2,1642939$$
$$\oplus = 2,5489126 = 353,9$$
$$x = 2,0612323$$
$$x^{1/2} = 1,0306161$$
$$8,4 = 0,9242793$$
$$k = 0,1063368 = 1,277$$

Logarithms

$$x = 2,0612323$$
$$3)\ 4,1224646$$
$$x^{2/3} = 1,3741548$$
$$18,8 = 1,2741578$$
$$d = 0,0999960 = 1,259$$
$$x^{1 + 1/20} = 2,1642939$$
$$z = 1,4798994$$
$$3,6441933$$
$$1,5 = 0,1760913$$
$$W = 3,4681020 = 2938$$
$$x^{23/20} = 2,3704171$$
$$43,2 = 1,6354837$$
$$V = 0,7349334 = 5,43$$
$$x^{11/20} = 1,1336777$$
$$2,147 = 0,3318320$$
$$S = 0,8018457 = 6,337$$
$$x^{11/20} = 1,1336777$$
$$30 = 1,4771213$$
$$30 \cdot x^{11/20} = 2,6107990 = 408,1$$
$$x^{23/20} = 2,3704171 = 234,6$$
$$2,2392995 = 173,5$$
$$64 = 1,8061800$$
$$L = 0,4331195 = 2,711$$
$$x^3 = 6,1836969$$
$$6,6168164$$
$$52 = 1,7160033$$
$$M = 4,9008131 = 79590$$

If we find it necessary to carry a certain quality to a greater degree than the proportions of the tables give, this alteration may be effected according to the principles laid down; but it must not be forgotten that we cannot improve one quality but at the expence of another. The table is so plain, that for its complete application, it only requires an example. Thus let there be required the proportions and dimensions of a bark of 200 lasts.

By a last is meant 18 skiponds iron weight; the skipond iron weight = 320 pounds; so that a last = 5760 pounds. A cubic foot of sea-water weighs 63 pounds; hence a last is nearly equal to 91 cubic feet of sea-water; so that 200 lasts = 18200 cubic feet of sea-water.

Thus it appears that a bark of 200 lasts ought to have 29350 cubic feet of displacement to the outside of the timbers; 115,14 feet in length from the stem to the stern-post; 30,19 feet of breadth to the outside of the timbers; 13,98 feet measured at the frame ⊕, from the load water-line to the upper edge of the rabbet of the keel; the surface of the frame ⊕ will be 353,9 square feet, the keel will have in depth from the upper edge of the rabbet 1,277 feet; there will be 1,259 difference of draught of water forward and aft; the surface of the load water-line will be 2938 square feet. The center of gravity of the displacement will be below the load water-line 5,43 feet; $\int \dfrac{\left[\begin{smallmatrix}2\\3\end{smallmatrix}\right] y^3 d\dot{x}}{D}$ or the distance of this center of gravity from the metacenter will be 6,337 feet; there will be between the metacenter and the common center of gravity of the ship and the lading, a distance of 2,711 feet; whence the moment of stability = 79590.

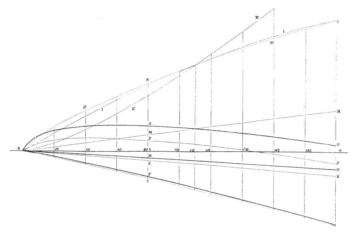

Fig. 32

To find immediately the properties of ships, proportioned according to table N°. 1, Figure 32 is constructed, where the numbers 20, 40, 60, &c. represent the length from the stem to the stern-post.

If AB be the load water-line for a bark, CCB is the locus of the center of gravity of displacement; DDB that of the metacenter; EEB that of the center of gravity of the ship and the lading. For a frigate, FFB is the locus of the center of gravity of the displacement; GGB that of the metacenter, HHB that of the ship with its lading. So that for a vessel of the form of a bark 80 feet long, the distance from the load water-line to the center of gravity of displacement = LC; the height of the metacenter above the load water-line = LD, this load water-line is above the center of gravity of the vessel with its lading by a quantity = LE.

But for a frigate, the distance of the center of gravity of the displacement below the water = LF, the height of the metacenter above the water = LG; the center of gravity of the ship and the lading is below the water by a quantity = LH. The line IIB determines the length the main-mast ought to have, so as to have the proper proportion according to the stability; that is to say, the length of the main-mast is as the distance of IIB from AB.

If there be given to large and small ships a form similar to that which is 110 feet in length, then the straight line MB will be the locus of the metacenter, and the other line KKB will determine the length of the main-mast, in the proportion required by the stability.

In determining the center of gravity of the ship and its lading, we have supposed the cargoes of ships to be similar; so that, if the bark of 80 feet in length has its center of gravity in E, the centers of gravity of other barks may be in the line EEB; in like manner, the centers of gravity of all frigates are in the line HHB.

On the proportions of privateers

Privateers are vessels, which an individual arms in time of war, by the authority of government, to take merchant ships and others belonging to the enemy.

In estimating the equipment of privateers, it must be considered, although some merchant ships are unable to make any resistance, that other large vessels may be encountered at sea, which are armed with guns. It is therefore necessary that privateers should be also well armed and have a sufficient crew, as well for action as for taking possession of their prizes.

For the attack of small ships the least privateers will do; but as these can only carry a few guns, the effect of which must be inconsiderable, their object should be to board; their principal force consists in the number of the crew.

If ships of superior force were not to be feared at sea, all sorts of ships might be employed in privateering, provided they were well armed with guns and men. But as a privateer may possibly meet with ships of the line, which are always of greater force, to escape in the chase, it should carry sail well, and sail fast in bad weather.

Independently of ships of the line, such a vessel is also liable to meet with frigates of war and privateers; with respect to privateers, as on each side they are armed by individuals, who have no other object but their own profit, it is not to be presumed that they will engage in a contest, from which nothing could result but mutual damage, without forwarding the views of their owners.

It is not so with frigates of war; their object is to attack and take, as much as possible, the enemy's privateers. If then a privateer cannot escape by its superiority of sailing (which since frigates are built to sail well is usually the case), it is necessary that it should be able to defend itself. The qualities of the vessel decide most frequently these combats. If the enemy be large and carry heavy guns, the privateer should also have them, and rather of a large caliber than in great number; which is more advantageous, not only on account of their greater effect, but also because there is a greater interval between the guns, so that the men at the oars and guns are not too much in the way of each other. These oars serve during the battle to present the privateer in an advantageous position, and in a calm to retire from a superior enemy. The privateer should sail well in all sorts of weather, and especially come about well; particularly, it should have a strong force in musketry, some small guns or swivels to fire case shot, and a good netting.

With respect to small privateers, as they are constantly forced to run from ships of war, their principal quality should consist in sailing well.

Besides the necessary qualities for action, the privateer ought to have a sufficient hold to carry stores, both of provisions and ammunition, for a cruise of a determined length, without sinking the vessel beyond a certain fixed depth.

Upon the whole it appears that the most advantageous qualities for a privateer are to sail fast, and to be sufficiently stiff to carry sail in bad weather.

We have seen in the previous chapter that to attain this object, it is necessary to give great length and breadth in proportion to the solidity of the immersed part. But as the construction of a ship of great length and of great breadth is very expensive, and requires a numerous crew to work it, it is not possible to carry these dimensions so far as might be wished; but one must be content with less than the greatest perfection in the property of sailing well, since the cost of the ship, with the pay and subsistence of the men, which amount to a great sum, would exceed the advantages gained. And as in constructing a privateer, certain views are entertained, which are to be carried into effect by a certain quantity of artillery, it is therefore the artillery, upon which the proportions ought to be founded.

The displacement of a ship, of which the size is known, as well as the weights it is to carry, may be found without difficulty; but it is not possible by theory alone, without the assistance of practical knowledge, to determine the true value, which the moment of stability ought to have.

By the comparison of different species of ships, it has been found, that privateers in general, large as well as small, have the proper stability, when the distance of their metacenter from the center of gravity of the ship is 6 feet; and since it is found that this center of gravity should be in the load water-line, the metacenter should be 6 feet above the load water-line.

The length, breadth, depth, and displacement, ought therefore to be so proportioned with respect to the guns and their position, that the center of gravity of the ship may be in the load water-line, and the metacenter 6 feet above.

But since these proportions, &c. cannot be found but by the means of approximation, to facilitate the investigation, I shall give hereafter general formulæ, which according to the weight, nature, and situation of the artillery, express the proportions of all kinds of privateers, from the largest frigate to the smallest sloop. For large vessels I have considered particularly the force of the artillery; with respect to the least, I have paid less attention to the artillery, than to the number of the crew, in which its whole force consists.

All vessels constructed from these proportions will be good sailers; and the smallest will sail equally well with the largest.

As the weight of the artillery and stores, which enter into the calculation and use of these formulæ, is the principal foundation thereof, I have thought proper to give the following table.

Weight of Guns and Stores proper for Privateers											
Pounders	Weight of a shot in provision weight	Numbers by which the weight of the shot is multiplied to find that of the gun	Weight of the gun		Numbers by which the weight of the gun is divided to find the weight of the carriage, &c.	Weight of the carriages, breechings and tackles	Weight of the shot, powder, wadding equal the weight of 126 shot	Weight of the guns, carriages, breechings, tackles, shot, powder, and wadding	A	Weight of the guns, carriages, breechings, and tackles	C
			Provision weight	Iron weight							
Caliber	pounds		pounds	Skip		pounds	pounds	pounds	Cubic ft. of water 63 lb. each foot	pounds	Cubic ft. of water 63 lb. each foot
24	29	215	6235	19,48	4,70	1326	3654	11215	178	7561	120
22	—	216	—	—	4,63	—	—	—	—	—	—
20	—	218	—	—	4,56	—	—	—	—	—	—
18	21,75	221	4807	15	4,49	1070	2740	8617	136,77	5877	93,3
16	—	225	—	—	4,42	—	—	—	—	—	—
14	—	230	—	—	4,35	—	—	—	—	—	—
12	14,5	236	3422	10,69	4,28	799	1827	6048	96	4221	67
10	—	243	—	—	4,21	—	—	—	—	—	—
8	9 2/3	251	2426	7,58	4,14	586	1218	4230	67,1	3012	47,8
6	7,25	260	1885	5,89	4,07	463	914	3262	51,77	2348	37,3
4	4,833	270	1305	4,07	4,00	326	609	2240	35,55	1631	25,9
3	3,625	276	1000	3,12	3,93	254	457	1711	27,16	1254	20,0
Swiv. 3	3,625	70	254	0,80	—	60	400	714	11,33	314	5,0
Swiv. 2	2,416	70	169	0,53	—	42	266	477	7,57	211	3,35

In the above table, the weight of the gun is proportioned to the weight of the shot; and in order to follow uniformly the law of the increasing proportion between the shot and the guns, as the latter become smaller, we have been induced to put in this table several sorts of guns, which are not in use.

To proportion the weight of the gun by that of the shot, is not certainly the best method; it should be determined by other circumstances; however for the object in view, we may allow this method of proceeding, especially since it gives a result very nearly approaching to the ordinary weight.

There is moreover in the table, in columns A and C, the weight of the guns, which must be multiplied by the number to be carried by the privateer, of which the plan is required. In the calculation, the whole weight of the guns is made equal to A or C.

It may be allowed that a 24 lb. shot weights 29 pounds provision weight, a cubic foot of iron of this kind weighing 440 pounds; the same proportion is observed for the other shot.

In the following calculations, it is estimated that the weight of a man is 170 pounds = 2,7 cubic feet of sea-water, supposing one foot to weigh 63 pounds; the weight of a man and his effects = 4 cubic feet; the casks, provisions, wood for cooking during a month = 189 pounds = 3 cubic feet, of sea-water; the water including the cask, for 15 days = 112 pounds = 1,78 cubic feet.

D = the displacement of the vessel to the outside of the timbers, B = the weight of the part above the water comprising the masts, yards, sails, rigging; a = the distance of the common center of gravity of these weights from the load water-line; c = the distance of the center of gravity of all the guns, also from load water-line. The center of gravity of the lower tier of guns is supposed to be one-third the height of the middle port from its lower sill. In like manner, the center of gravity of the guns on the quarter-deck and forecastle is taken one-third of the height of the foremost port on the quarter-deck. For the center of gravity of the swivels, we take that of the middle swivel, z = the breadth of the ship to the outside of the timbers, y = the half breadth, and x = the length from the forepart of the stem to the aft part of the stern-post; d = the depth of the ship taken at the frame $\oplus$, from the load water-line to the rabbet of the keel.

We may also estimate the number of the crew to be = $3{,}763\,A^{5/9}$, of which the weight is = $10{,}16\,A^{5/9}$, and with their effects = $15\,A^{5/9}$. The provisions for k months, and water for half the time, casks, wood, &c. included = $18 \times kA^{5/9}$.

To be able to observe a certain order between these ships, we have supposed the largest provisioned for a longer time than the small ones, consequently, we may make $k = \dfrac{A^{2/7}}{2{,}756}$, whence $18 \times k \times A^{5/9} = 6{,}534 \times A^{53/63}$. If all the weights $15\,A^{5/9} + 6{,}534\,A^{53/63} + A = K$, the displacement will be well proportioned, D being = $6{,}84 \times c^{1/4} \times K^{13/15}$. Then we may make the weight $B = \dfrac{D^{21/20}}{6{,}281}$, and the distance $a = \dfrac{D^{1/3}}{3{,}48}$.

Make $C + 10{,}16 \times A^{5/9} = Q$, and let the center of gravity of displacement be below the load water-line by an unknown quantity m; the moment of stability will be expressed by $\dfrac{2}{3}\int y^3\dot{x} - (m+a) \times B - (m+c) \times Q$; but since $\dfrac{2}{3}\int y^3\dot{x} = (m+6) \times D$, then accordingly $(m+6) \times D - (m+a) \times B - (m+c) \times Q = 6D$; hence

$$m = \frac{aB + cQ}{D - (B+Q)}.$$

It is necessary to take care in making a plan, that the center of gravity of the part immersed does not descend lower than this quantity; it would be better that it should be higher; for by making it lower, the stability will be diminished; the contrary will take place, if it be raised.

We have also found that $(m+6) \times D$, or $\dfrac{2}{3}\int y^3\dot{x}$ may be = $\dfrac{z^3 x^{21/20}}{26}$, and $z = \dfrac{x^{9/10}}{2{,}36}$; hence $(m+6) \times D = \dfrac{x^{15/4}}{341{,}8}$, and thus $x = \left(341{,}8 \times (m+6) \times D\right)^{4/15}$. The area of the load water-line should be = $\dfrac{z x^{24/23}}{1{,}626}$, and the area of the frame $\oplus = \dfrac{2{,}366 \times D}{x^{13/12}}$; also $d = \dfrac{x}{10{,}5}$. The center of gravity of the ballast is supposed to be below the plane of the load water-line by a quantity = $\dfrac{x^{7/5}}{95}$, and the weight of the ballast =

$$95 \times \left\{ \frac{1{,}11 \times \left((m+a) \times B + (m+c) \times Q\right) - mD}{x^{7/5} - 95\,m} \right\}.$$

We have found that the moment of the sails, in respect to the center of gravity of the ship or to the load water-line, should be = $\dfrac{35{,}56 \times 6D}{x^{1/3}}$.

As to the length x, which we have found here, it might be varied according to the distance between the guns, the disposition of the rowports, and the accommodations; this length, however, must not be much altered, if it be wished that the value of $\dfrac{2}{3}\int y^3\dot{x}$ should remain constant.

For a better guide, the following is the least distance, which can be allowed between the guns from center to center; for 24 pounders 10 1/3 feet; 8 pounders 8 5/6 feet; 4 pounders 7 11/12 feet; 18 pounders 9 5/6 feet; 6 pounders 8 1/3 feet; 3 pounders 7 1/2 feet; 12 pounders 9 1/3 feet.

But if it be wished to make two row-ports between each gun, the distance from gun-port to gun-port cannot be less than 8 feet.

The first port forward may be placed, so that the after side may be abreast of the center of the foremast; or that the foreside may be a little abast the after side of the foremast.

It is necessary to set off the distance between the after-port and the stern-post, one distance between the ports and one breadth of a port, more or less, according to the disposition of the accommodations.

It is proper in this place to insert the proportions of the ports, which experience has proved to be the best.

Pounders	Height of the Sills above the Decks	Height of the Ports	Breadth of the Ports
	Inches	Inches	Inches
24 pounds	28	34	40
18 ,,	26	31	36
12 ,,	24	28	33
8 ,,	22	25	30
6 ,,	20	22	27
4 ,,	18	19	24
3 ,,	16	17	21

For greater clearness, I give below the expressions in the order in which they should be employed in the calculations.

Formulæ for the proportions of Privateers.

$$15\, A^{5/9} + 6{,}534\, A^{53/63} + A = K$$

$$6{,}84 \times c^{1/4} \times K^{13/15} = D$$

$$\frac{D^{21/20}}{6{,}281} = B, \quad \frac{D^{1/3}}{3{,}48} = a, \quad 10{,}16\, A^{5/9} + C = Q$$

$$\frac{aB + cQ}{D - (B + Q)} = m$$

$$\text{weight of ballast} = 95 \times \frac{\left(1{,}11 \times (\overline{m + a} \times B + \overline{m + c} \times Q) - mD\right)}{x^{7/5} - 95\, m}$$

$$341{,}8 \times (m + 6) \times D^{4/15} = x$$

$$\frac{x^{9/10}}{2{,}36} = z, \quad \frac{z x^{24/23}}{1{,}626} = \text{area of the load water-line.}$$

$$\frac{2{,}366 \times D}{x^{13/12}} = \text{area of section } \oplus, \quad \frac{x}{10{,}5} = d$$

$$3{,}763 \times A^{5/9} = \text{the number of the crew}, \quad \frac{A^{2/7}}{2{,}756} = k \text{ months provisions.}$$

The distance which the center of gravity of the ballast is below the load water-line $= \dfrac{x^{7/5}}{95}$. The difference of the draught of water fore and aft $= \dfrac{x^{5/8}}{14{,}46}$.

The moment of the sails from the load water-line $= \dfrac{35{,}56 \times 6D}{x^{1/3}}$.

To facilitate the use of the formula according to the number of guns, their caliber, and the height of the battery, the following table has been constructed of the values of A, C, &c. for 16 privateers carrying different numbers of guns.

| Num-ber of the Ship | Guns | | | | Height of the battery | Height of the ports | A third of the height of the ports | Dist. of center of gravity of guns of 1st battery from load water-line | Distance between the batteries | Weight of the first battery with carriages, breechings, and tackles, &c. | Weight of the upper battery with carriages, &c. | Quantity C | Common center of gravity of all the guns above load water-line, or c | Quantity A |
| | First Battery | | Second Battery, or that of quarter deck, and forecastle | | | | | | | | | | | |
	No.	Caliber	No.	Caliber	Feet	Feet	Feet	Feet	Feet	Cubic ft.	Cubic ft.	Cubic ft.	Feet	Cubic ft.
1	28	18	12	6	8,5	2,58	0,86	9,36	6,4	2612,4	447,6	3060	10,29	4451
2	26	18	10	6	7	2,58	0,86	7,86	6,3	2425,8	373	2799	8,69	4074
3	26	12	10	4	6,5	2,33	0,77	7,28	6,2	1742	259	2001	8,08	2851
4	24	12	8	4	6	2,33	0,77	6,78	6,1	1608	207,2	1815	7,47	2588
5	24	8	8	3	5,75	2,08	0,69	6,44	6,0	1147,2	160	1307	6,85	1827
6	22	8			5,5	2,08	0,69	6,19		1051,6		1052	6,19	1476
7	22	6			5,25	1,83	0,61	5,86		820,6		821	5,86	1139
8	20	6			5	1,83	0,61	5,61		746,0		746	5,61	1035
9	18	6			4,75	1,83	0,61	5,36		671,4		671	5,36	932
10	16	6			4,5	1,83	0,61	5,11		596,8		597	5,11	828
11	14	6			4,25	1,83	0,61	4,86		522,2		522	4,86	725
12	12	6			4	1,83	0,61	4,61		447,6		448	4,61	621
13	10	6			3,75	1,83	0,61	4,36		373,0		373	4,36	518
14	8	6	Swiv.		3,5	1,83	0,61	4,11		298,4		298	4,11	414
15	1	12	16	3	4			4,5		147,0		147	4,50	277
16	1	18	16	2	3,75			4,0		101,4		101,4	4,00	188

Suppose it is required to make a plan for a privateer of 24 twelve pounders on the main deck, 8 four pounders on the quarter deck and fore-castle, with six feet battery, or the lowest sill of the middle gun port 6 feet above the water; this is the privateer number 4 of the table, so that there will be for A, C and c the following values.

By this process it will be found, that the privateer of 24 twelve pounders on the main deck, of 8 four pounders on the quarter deck and forecastle, and having the sill of the middle port of the lowest battery 6 feet above the water, should have 29140 cubic feet of displacement outside the timbers, not including the keel, the stem, and the stern-post.

The center of gravity of the said displacement will be below the plane of the load water-line   4,595 feet

$$\frac{2}{3}\int y^3 \dot{x} = 311600$$

The length from the stem to the stern-post 138,24

The breadth to the outside of the timbers 35,78

Ballast in cubic feet of sea-water 2616

Area of the load water-line 3769   square feet

Depth of the frame $\oplus$ from load water-line to rabbet of keel .... 13,16 feet

Area of frame $\oplus$ .... 330,7 square feet

Number of crew 296   men

Months for which provisioned 3,46

Quantity by which the center of gravity of the ballast should be below load water-line ... 10,45 feet

Difference of the draught of water .... 1,51 feet

Moment of sails from the center of gravity of the ship, or from the load water-line.......... 1202400

$$A = 2588, C = 1815, c = 7{,}47; \quad \log. 7{,}47 = 0{,}8733206; \quad \log. c^{1/4} = 02183301$$

Logarithms (left column)

$A = 2588$ log. $= 3{,}4129643$

$A^{5/9}$ .... $= 1{,}8960913$

15 .... $= 1{,}1760913$ N. N^r.

$15\,A^{5/9}$ .... $= 3{,}0721826 = 1180{,}8$

$A^{53/63}$ .... $= 2{,}8712239$

$6{,}534$ .... $= 0{,}8151791 \quad A = 2588$

$\qquad\qquad\qquad\quad 3{,}6864030 \qquad = \underline{4858}$

K .... $= 3{,}9358598 \qquad 8627$

$K^{13/15}$ .... $= 3{,}4110785$

$c^{1/4}$ .... $= 0{,}2183301$

$6{,}84$ .... $= 0{,}8350561$

D .... $= 4{,}4644647 = 29140$

$D^{20/21}$ .... $= 4{,}6876879$

$6{,}281$ .... $= 0{,}7980288$

B .... $= 3{,}8896591 = 7756$

$D^{1/3}$ .... $= 1{,}4881549$

$3{,}48$ .... $= 0{,}5415792$

a .... $= 0{,}9465757 = 8{,}842$

B .... $= 3{,}8896591$

$a\,B$ .... $= 4{,}8362348 = 68590$

$A^{5/9}$ .... $= 1{,}8960913$

$10{,}16$ .... $= 1{,}0068937 \quad C = 1815$

$10{,}16\,A^{5/9}$ .... $= 2{,}9029850 = \underline{799{,}8}$

Q .... $= 3{,}4174717 = 2615$

c .... $= 0{,}8733206$

$c\,Q$ .... $= 4{,}2907923 = \underline{19534}$

$a\,B + c\,Q$ .... $= 4{,}9450750 = 88124$

$D - (B + Q)$ .... $= 4{,}2734411 = 18769$

m .... $= 0{,}6716339 = 4{,}695$

$m + a$ .... $= 1{,}1315224 = 13{,}537$

B .... $= 3{,}8896591$

$(m + a)\,B$ .... $= 5{,}0211815 = 105000$

$m + c$ .... $= 1{,}0851121 = 12{,}165$

Q .... $= 3{,}4174717$

$(m + c)\,Q$ .... $= 4{,}5025838 = \underline{31810}$

$\qquad\qquad\qquad\quad 5{,}1361178 = 136810$

$1{,}11$ .... $= 0{,}0453230$

$\qquad\qquad\qquad\quad 5{,}1814408 = 151860$

D .... $= 4{,}4644647$

m .... $= 0{,}6716339$

$m\,D$ .... $= 5{,}1360986 = 136800$

$\qquad\qquad\qquad\quad 4{,}1778250 = 15060$

95 .... $= 1{,}9777236$

$\qquad\qquad\qquad\quad 6{,}1555486$

Logarithms (right column)

$x^{7/5}$ .... $= 2{,}9969025 = 992{,}9$

95 .... $= 1{,}9777236$

m .... $= 0{,}6716339$

$95\,m$ .... $= 2{,}6493575 = 446$

$\qquad\qquad\qquad\quad 2{,}7379079 = 546{,}9$

Ballast .... $= 3{,}4176407 = 2616$

D .... $= 4{,}4644647$

$m + 6$ .... $= 1{,}0291808 = 10{,}695$

$\int \frac{2}{3}\, y^3 x$ .... $= 5{,}4936455 = 311600$

$341{,}8$ .... $= 2{,}5337721$

$\qquad\qquad\qquad\quad 8{,}0274176$

x .... $= 2{,}1406447 = 138{,}24$

$x^{9/10}$ .... $= 1{,}9265803$

$2{,}36$ .... $= 0{,}3729120$

z .... $= 1{,}5536683 = 35{,}78$

$x^{24/23}$ .... $= 2{,}2337162$

$\qquad\qquad\qquad\quad 3{,}7873845$

$1{,}626$ .... $= 0{,}2111205$

Area of load water-line . $= 3{,}5762640 = 3769$

d .... $= \dfrac{138{,}24}{10{,}5} = 13{,}16$

D .... $= 4{,}4644647$

$2{,}366$ .... $= 0{,}3740147$

$\qquad\qquad\qquad\quad 4{,}8384794$

$x^{13/12}$ .... $= 2{,}3190317$

Area of $\oplus$ .... $= 2{,}5194477 = 330{,}7$

$A^{5/9}$ .... $= 1{,}8960913$

$3{,}763$ .... $= 0{,}5755342$

Crew .... $= 2{,}4716255 = 296$

$A^{2/7}$ .... $= 0{,}9751326$

$2{,}756$ .... $= 0{,}4402792$

(k) .... $= 0{,}5348534 = 3{,}426$

$x^{7/5}$ .... $= 2{,}9969025$

95 .... $= 1{,}9777236$

Ballast below water .... $= 1{,}0191789 = 10{,}45$

$x^{5/8}$ .... $= 1{,}3379029$

$14{,}46$ .... $= 1{,}1601683$

Diff. of draught of water $= 0{,}1777346 = 1{,}506$

$6\,D$ .... $= 5{,}2426408 = 174840$

$35{,}56$ .... $= 1{,}5509618$

$\qquad\qquad\qquad\quad 6{,}7936026$

$x^{1/3}$ .... $= 0{,}7135482$

Moment of the sails ... $= 6{,}0800544 = 1202400$

If the artillery had been planned otherwise, or if it were necessary to place the battery lower or higher, the proportions of the frigate would not be the same: however, it may be observed, that this height of the battery does not differ far from what is in common use.

To shew more sensibly the difference of form between small and great ships, which are constructed according to the proportions given according to the formulæ, Figure 34 is constructed, which is to be understood in the following manner:

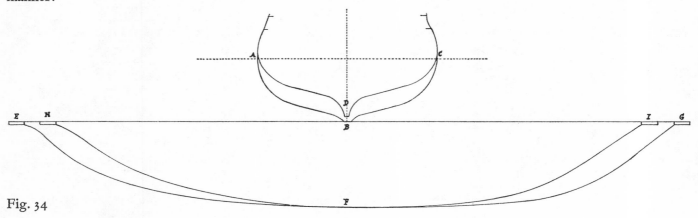

Fig. 34

ABC is the midship bend of a privateer 138¼ feet in length, and 35¾ in breadth; *ADC* is the frame ⊕ of a small privateer or boat 44¾ feet in length, and 13 feet in breadth, and *AC* is the load water-line; and according to the proportion, which there should be between the length and breadth, *EFG* will be the load water-line of the large privateer, and *HFI* that of the small one. These elements being known, it will not be difficult, with some knowledge of construction, and a little practice, to draw plans, which, every thing being well attended to, will differ little from those given in my *Architectura Navalis*, since the formulæ have been calculated after those plans; or to speak more correctly, they have been employed conjointly with others, in finding these different expressions.

I do not pretend to say, however, that one ought always to observe these proportions. Different cases present themselves, which may require different alterations: for instance, to navigate in seas where the waves are short and high, ships, particularly small ones, should have more breadth in proportion to the length.

In like manner, different kinds of rigging require alterations in the proportions: if the vessel be schooner rigged, it is necessary that it should have a greater relative length to allow a proper extent to the sails in proportion to the stability; the rigging of sloops on the contrary requires more breadth in proportion to the length.

There are privateers, which are obliged to go out to sea to meet with prizes; others have no occasion to go far from the coast; these two kinds ought to be provisioned differently; the one requires greater capacity than the other, although they may be of the same force, a circumstance which will necessarily cause differences in the principal dimensions; regarding it as an invariable principle, that the center of gravity of the ship with its lading, should be in the plane of the load water-line, and the metacenter 6 feet above.

As far as regards the accommodations, their distribution may be partly seen in the plans of my *Architectura Navalis*; but the size of the ships, and also the climates where they are meant to navigate, must influence greatly the nature of the accommodations.

Ships sufficiently large and stable should have large gangways, whereon to place the musketry, and they ought to be well netted on the gunwales.

In hot climates, ships should be more open, especially, if they are not liable to be sent on expeditions of long duration; but in cold climates, care should be taken that the crews be well sheltered: so that, in large privateer ships, instead of wide gangways, it would be more convenient to extend the quarter-deck and forecastle, with large gratings in the middle for the passage of the smoke in action. These gratings should be covered with tarpawlings in bad weather.

In some countries, they have their cables in the hold; in others, between decks; both methods have advantages and inconveniences. There are also different customs for the hours of meals, and for their galleys; some cook thrice a day; others cook only once: all this requires in a ship different arrangements, and what is right for one, is not convenient for the other.

Hence we see, how necessary it is to be acquainted with all these, and many other similar circumstances, before a draught is begun; and that it afterwards requires judgment and practice in the business, in order to arrange and adapt rightly, and according to circumstances, every particular thing; so as to include all possible conveniences, to have room to work the ship, and to avoid crowding.

On the proportions of masts and yards for merchant ships

The proportions then of masts and yards are founded on the length and breadth of ships in the following manner. As the breadth of ships has the greatest influence on the stability, the lower masts and top-masts should be proportioned to the breadth, whence not only the height of the sails, but moreover the height of their common center of gravity, will be in proportion to the said breadth; as to the breadth of the sails, or what is the same thing, the length of the yards, it should be proportioned to the length of the ship: thence it follows, that the moment of the sails will be as the square of the breadth, multiplied by the length. Small ships then will have a greater moment of canvass in proportion to the stability, than large ones; which agrees with what was observed above concerning the area of canvass for small ships: and it is a received custom for small ships, to increase the height of the lower masts still more, but at the same time to diminish that of the top-masts. The height of the main-mast of a trading ship with three masts, its breadth being $= B$, is $= 3,23 \, B^{11/12}$, and the height of the main top-mast, reckoning from the upper side of the cross-trees, that of the main-mast being $= L$, is $\dfrac{L^{11/10}}{2,73}$ for frigates, and $\dfrac{L^{11/10}}{2,84}$ for barks. The relation of the masts, proportioned according to this method, to the masts proportioned according to the stability, may be seen by Fig. 32, where the line BNN determines the height of the masts in the proportion of $B^{11/12}$.

The length of the bowsprit outside of the stem, for frigates, is $1,15 \times$ the breadth of the ship, and for barks $1,1 \times$ the said breadth.

It is not sufficient to study merely to regulate the height of the masts, and the length of the yards, by the size of the ships; but also to use those which have such a proportion among themselves, that all the rigging may make a handsome appearance.

That the ships may be well rigged, it is necessary in the first place, that the fore-stay and main topmast-stay should be in a straight line, in like manner, the main-stay and the mizen topmast-stay: the fore-stay may end on the bowsprit, between one-third and two-fifths of its length from the small end; secondly, that the top-sails should be of similar figures, or at least, that their sides should be of the same cut; thirdly, that when the ship is seen, at one or the other of the extremities, the shrouds and the breast back-stays should appear parallel: this depends partly on the breadth of the channels, which ought to be regulated in a manner conducive to this end. To effect this, the length of the head of the main-mast, from the under side of the trestle-trees, which is 5/36 of the length of the said mast, being $= T$, the cap of the fore-mast should be lower than that of the main-mast by a quantity $= 2,22 \times T^{1/3}$ for frigates, and $= 2 \times T^{1/4}$ for barks. The cap of the mizen-mast should be on a level with the main-top.

If the length of the main top-mast $= S$, the length of the mizen top-mast will be $= 1,3 \times S^{6/7}$ for frigates, and $= 1,316 \times S^{6/7}$ for barks, supposing the length of the pole to be in the same proportion, as for the other top-masts; if it be longer, then that difference is added more.

The head of the mizen-mast ought to be 3/4, and that of the fore-mast 9/10 of that of the main-mast. The length of the fore top-mast should also be 9/10 of that the main; the head of these masts 1/9 or 2/17 of their length. The length of the top-gallant masts to the stop $= 0,54 \times$ the length of the top-mast; the length of the main yard $= 0,52 \times$ the length of the ship from the stem to the stern-post for frigates, and the main top-sail yard $= 0,79 \times$ by the length of the main yard; as for barks, the length from end to end being $= L$, the length of the main yard will be $= 0,6 \times L^{20/21}$; and the length of the main top-sail yard will be $= 0,81 \times$ by the length of the main yard. The main top-gallant yard $= 0,7 \times$ by the length of the main top-sail yard. All the yards of the fore mast are 9/10 of those the main-mast.

The proportion of the mizen top-sail yard to its mast, is equal to the proportion of the main top-sail yard to the main top-mast: the cross-jack yard $= 1,22 \times$ the length of the mizen top-sail yard for frigates, and $= 1,18 \times$ this length for barks. The sprit-sail yard $=$ the fore top-sail yard; the sprit-sail top-sail yard $=$ the fore-top-gallant yard.

The yard arms are 1/11 of their length for the lower yards, and those of the top-gallant yards; but 1/7 for the top-sail yards.

The distance of the center of gravity of the fore-mast from the perpendicular at the stem is 4/31 of the length. The center of the main-mast is 2/31 behind the middle of the ship. The distance of the center of the mizen-mast from the perpendicular at the stern-post is $= 0,182 \times$ by the length of the ship.

The main-mast should rake aft one foot in thirty; the mizen-mast should have double the rake of the main-mast; the fore-mast should be perpendicular; the elevation of the bowsprit, above the horizontal plane, should be in a length of 7 feet, about 4 feet for frigates, and 3 feet for barks.

It is according to these proportions that the masts and yards may be initially calculated; it will be however necessary, when the dimensions of the masts are given for the ship, to make a rigging draught, in order to proportion one according to the other, so that the whole may make a handsome appearance.

As to the diameter, experience has shewn that if the length of the main-mast, the main-yard and the main top-mast are denoted by L, R, and S feet, the diameter of the main-mast in inches will be $\dfrac{L \times R^{1/3}}{13}$; that of the main top-mast will be $\dfrac{S^{11/10}}{4,68}$; the diameter of the fore-mast will be 1/20 less than that of the main-mast; and the diameter of the fore top-mast will be 1/20 less than that of the main top-mast. The diameter of the top-gallant mast $= 0,3 \times$ their length reckoning to the stop.

The diameter of the bowsprit will be a mean between that of the main-mast and that of the fore-mast; the diameter of the jib-boom will be 3/4 of that of the main top-mast. The diameter of the mizen-mast 2/3 of that of the main-mast, and the diameter of the mizen top-mast 2/3 of that of the main top-mast.

The diameter of the main-yard, and that of the fore-yard in inches $= 0,25 \times$ the length of the yard; that of the top-sail yards $= 0,23 \times$ also by the length of the yards; that of the top-gallant yard $= 1/6$ of their length. The diameters of the sprit-sail yard, and cross-jack yard $= 0,21$ the length. The diameter of the sprit-sail top-sail yard $=$ that of the main top-gallant yard. The diameter of the mizen peak is an inch for four feet in its length. The studding sail booms have two feet greater length than half the yard, and their diameter in inches is 1/5 or 1/6 of their length in feet.

The depth of the main-trestle-trees in inches is the fourth of the height of the top-mast in feet, less half an inch; the thickness of the fore-trestle trees is 1/16 less than that of the main-trestle-trees, and the mizen 3/5 of the main; the thickness of the top-mast cross-trees is 3/7 that of the trestle-trees of the respective tops. The breadth of the said trestle-trees and cross-trees is 5/7 or 3/4 of their depth.

The thickness of the caps is 4/5 of the diameters of the top-masts.

As the masts and yards taper towards their extremities, it is not sufficient to have their greatest diameters, it is necessary also to know the proportion according to which they are diminished, for the purpose of giving them the form which according to experience affords sufficient strength to sustain the efforts to which they are exposed. The distance between the greatest and least diameters is divided into four parts; the diameter at each of these divisions should be as follows.

The lower masts are found to be well proportioned when they have their diameter, at the height of the trestle-trees, one-eighth less than at the deck. So that, the diameter at the deck being 128, at the first division it will be 127, at the second 124, at the third 119, and at the fourth 112. The thickness within the trestle-trees will be 4/5, and above at the head, 5/8 of the diameter at the deck.

The top-masts have 1/5 less diameter under the cross-trees than at the cap of the lower masts. So that, the diameter at the cap being 80, at the first division it will be 79, at the second 76, at the third 71, and at the fourth, below the cross-trees 64. The thickness within the cross-trees and above at the head, will be 5/9 of the diameter at the cap.

If the great diameter of the lower and top-sail yards be 27, at the first division it will be 26, at the second 23, at the third 18, and at the outer end 11.

If the great diameter of the top-gallant yards is 32, at the first division it will be 31, at the second 28, at the third 23, and at the yard-arm 16.

The bowsprit has commonly at the outer end a diameter only one half of that at the gammoning; if the diameter at the gammoning is 60, at the first division it will be 59, at the second 55, at the third 46, and at the fourth 30.

Brigs and snows have their fore-masts and its appendages, as well as the bowsprit, of the same proportions as frigates. But the height of the main-mast of brigs ought to be such, that its top may be on a level with the cap of the fore-mast; the head of the main-mast is equal to the head of the fore-mast. The main top-mast is of the same length with the fore top-mast, the main yard and main top-mast yard are the same with the fore yard and fore-top mast yard.

In snows, the main-mast is a mean between the main-masts of a frigate and brig, so also the top-masts; but the main yard and the main top-sail yard, are of the same dimensions with those of frigates.

The length of the main-mast of schooners and galeasses to the hounds, ought to be thrice the breadth of the vessels; and in howker sloops the whole of the main-mast ought to be thrice their breadth.

The proportions for other masts and yards, as also for all of them, in small vessels, will be found in the draughts of Plate LXII. *Architectura Navalis*. The yards have there their half length.

East India ships have the length of the main-mast = 2,43 × their breadth; the length of the main top-mast = 0,586 × into that of the main-mast; the length of the main-yard = 0,54 × the length of the ship; the topsail-yard 0,8 × the main-yard; the main top-gallant yard 0,7 × by the top-sail yard; the mizen top-mast 3/4 of the fore top-mast.

The cap of the fore-mast is 2/5 of the length of the head of the main-mast lower than the cap of the main-mast; the cap of the mizen-mast is on a level with the main top. The other masts or yards are proportioned like those of merchant vessels frigate built.

In privateers the masts and yards are first proportioned, as for East India ships, after which a draught of them is made, in which are included the rigging and sails; lastly, their moment is compared with that of the stability, and the masts and yards will be determined, which are suitable to the moment of the sails.

On the construction of the scale of solidity

Suppose we wish to make the scale of solidity for the privateer (N°. 6, Plate XXXII), of which we have the displacement.

The calculation for the construction of this scale must commence from the plane of the load water-line, so as to obtain in succession the solidity between this and each of the lower water-lines; the operation is performed in the following manner.

To find the solidity of the part between the first and second water-lines.

Half the area of the load water-line	1293,91
Ditto of the second	1178,03
	2)2471,92
	1235,97
Multiplied by the distance between the water-lines	1,62
Half the solidity between the first and second water-lines	2002,27
Plank	50,73
Stem and stern-post	2,00
	2055,00 cubic feet
	2
Displacement of the part 1,62 feet below the load water-line	4110,00 = 45,16 lasts.

To find the solidity of the parts between the first and third water-lines.

Half the area of the load water-line	= 1293,91 × 1 = 1293,91
Ditto for the second	= 1178,03 × 4 = 4712,12
Ditto for the third	= 1030,69 × 1 = 1030,69
	7036,72
Multiplied by one-third the distance between the water-lines	0,54
Half the solidity between the first and third water-lines	3799,83
Plank	104,17
Stem and stern-post	4,00
	3908,00 cubic feet
	2
Displacement of the part 3,24 feet below the load water-line	7816,00 = 85,89 lasts.

To find the solidity of the pieces between the first and fourth water-lines.

Half the area of the third water-line	1030,69
Ditto of the fourth	856,93
	2)1887,62
	943,81
Multiplied by the distance between the water-lines	1,62
Half the solid between the third and fourth water-lines	1528,97
Half the solid between the first and third water-lines	3799,83
Half the solid between the first and fourth water-lines	5328,80
Plank	165,20
Stem and stern-post	6,00
	5500,00 cubic feet
	2
Displacement of the part 4,86 feet below the load water-line	11000,00 = 120,88 lasts

To find the solidity of the pieces between the first and fifth water-lines.

Half the area of the load water-line	= 1293,91 × 1 = 1293,91
Ditto of the second	= 1178,03 × 4 = 4712,12
Ditto of the third	= 1030,69 × 2 = 2061,38
Ditto of the fourth	= 854,93 × 4 = 4327,72
Ditto of the fifth	= 662,38 × 1 = 662,38
	12157,51
Multiplied by one-third the distance between the water-lines	0,54
Half the solidity between the first and fifth water-lines	6565,05
Plank	239,95
Stem and stern-post	9,00
	6814,00 cubic feet
	2
Displacement of the part 6,48 feet below the load water-line	13628,00 = 149,75 lasts.

To find the solidity of the pieces between the first and sixth water-lines.

Half the area of the fifth water-line	662,38
Ditto of the sixth	434,83
	2)1097,21
	548,60
Multiplied by the distance between the water-lines	1,62
	888,73
Half the solidity between the first and fifth water-lines	6565,05
Half the solidity between the first and sixth water-lines	7453,78
Plank	335,22
Stem and stern-post	12,00
	7801,00 cubic feet
	2
Displacement of the part 8,1 feet below the load water-line	15602,00 = 171,45 lasts

To find the solidity of the pieces between the first and seventh water-lines.

Half the solidity between the first and seventh water-line	7957
Plank	426
Stem and stern-post	16
	8399 cubic feet
	2
Displacement of the part 9,72 feet below the load water-line	16798 = 184,6 lasts.

To find the solidity from the load water-line to the keel.

Half the solidity between first water-line and the keel	8105
Plank	500
Stem and stern-post	20
Displacement of the part 11,72 feet below the load water-line	8625 cubic feet
	2
	17250 = 189,56 lasts.

To construct from hence a scale of burden.

Draw two lines perpendicular to each other, the one in a horizontal direction, the other in a vertical direction; make on the horizontal line a decimal scale at pleasure to represent lasts, and on the vertical another scale of feet also at pleasure, as is seen in Plate IV.

Below the horizontal line and at the distance from this superior line of 1.62, 3.24, 4.28, 6.48, 8.1, 9.72 and 11.2 feet, draw parallels thereto.

On the scale of lasts, take the quantities, which have been found, in lasts 45.16, 85.89, 120.88, 149.75, 171.45, 184.6 and 189.58; set off these quantities on the corresponding horizontal lines, from the vertical line.

Through all the points so determined pass a curve, and you will have a scale of solidity.

The horizontal scale is in French tons, English tons, and Swedish lasts.

The vertical scale, at right angles to the horizontal one and marked *S*, *E*, and *F*, is in Swedish, English and French feet. The curves marked No 1, No 2, No 3 etc., all of which meet at *e*, determine the burden of the vessels No. 1, 2, 3 etc. on Plates I, II, III, IV, V, VI and VII.

The method of using the scale is this.

The line *ab* on the sheer plan is the load water-line, the privateer being laden. Suppose that the water-line before it is entirely laden, were *cd*; then the distances *ac*, *bd* are taken, which by the scale of the plan give 4 feet 1 1/2 inches and 5 feet 1 1/2 inches; these two quantities are added, and half the sum is taken, 4 feet 7 1/2 inches.

Take this quantity 4 feet 7 1/2 inches on the scale of solidity, you will have *eg*, which must be transferred perpendicularly to the line *ef*, until it meet the curve in *h*. From *h* draw the line *hi* perpendicularly to *fe*, or what is the same thing, parallel to *eg*; this line marks on the scale of lading the weight, which must be put on board to bring down the ship to the line *ab*, namely, 175 Swedish lasts.

If the ship be quite light, one may in this manner find the lading, which it can take; or if the water-line of a ship has been once observed, supposing another to be found, one may be able, by means of the said scale, to obtain the weight which the ship has taken on board, or of which it has been discharged, to render it so much more brought down, or more raised.

If similar scales were made by builders for all ships and vessels constructed by them, the owner or commander would have it always in his power to determine the lading he could take on board, and that with such exactness as not to be deceived one last in the largest ship, when the load water-line was determined.

This scale is particularly necessary for ships of war or privateers, to the end that knowing the quantity of provisions and other stores, which they can take, the ballast may be determined, which they can receive without being brought down farther than the load water-line.

On the measurement for tonnage

By measurement for tonnage is meant the taking of the dimensions of a ship, in order, from the consideration of its form, to find the lading it can carry, and with which it can navigate without danger.

To measure for tonnage in the Swedish manner, is to determine the number of lasts, which the ship can carry, as follows.

The length of the ship is taken on the upper deck from the stem to the sternpost, the breadth within the ceiling, and the draught of water from the plank of the said upper deck to the plank of the bottom, these three dimensions are multiplied together, and the product is divided by 200; the five-sixths of the quotient will be the weight, which the ship can take in lasts of 18 skiponds iron weight *per* last; as much *per cent.* however is subtracted from this quantity as the measurer judges the ship more or less full in the floors, or as it carries a greater or less number of guns. The remainder is the burthen in lasts.

It follows from hence that if two ships were constructed from the same plan, but the upper deck of the one placed one foot higher than that of the other, the former would be found of a greater quantity of lasts than the latter; which ought however to be the contrary, for the former ship ought to carry less, as its sides being raised a foot weigh more (the two ships being laden to the same draught of water). The result of this calculation may moreover be erroneous on this account, that the degrees of the ship's rising, more or less, will not be always estimated correctly by a person in the hold; whence it happens that the addition or subtraction on this account must be in a great measure arbitrary; without mentioning other reasons, which render the measurement for tonnage, by this method, very uncertain.

If a last were a certain space, this manner of measuring would be more tolerable, but as it is a weight, it is altogether without reason.

The method of measuring for tonnage in England, is not used for the direct purpose of finding the quantity of lasts which the ship can carry, but to obtain the content, according to which the ship pays the duties.

The capacity is found thus: the product of the length of the keel multiplied by the breadth of the ship to the outside of the plank, and again by the half breadth; this product, I say, divided by 94, gives the capacity of the ship in tons. If the ship carries more than this quantity, it is said to carry more than its measurement for tonnage, and *vice versâ.*

Little need be said in regard to this method, because the immediate object of it is not to find the burthen; however the manner of determining the length of the keel, upon which length the calculation is founded, is faulty; 3/5 and 1/8 of the breadth of the ship are taken, for the rake of the stem and stern-post; these two quantities are subtracted from the length taken from the aft side of the wing transom at the middle line; the remainder is considered as the length of the keel. That this method is erroneous appears as follows.

Let the length of the ship from the stem to the stern-post equal m, and its breadth $= n$; then the length of the keel $= m - \left(\frac{3}{5} + \frac{1}{8}\right) \times n$. And as $\frac{3}{5} + \frac{1}{8}$ make nearly $\frac{3}{4}$, one may say that the measurement of the ship in tons, by the preceding rule, will be $= \dfrac{(m - 3/4\, n) \times 1/2\, n^2}{94}$. If this expression be made $= 0$, then the tonnage of the ship is equal to 0; it could therefore carry nothing. It is true, that to make this the case, the breadth of the ship must be 4/3 of the length, which is never the case.

Since when a ship is built by contract, it is usual to give so much *per* ton, it would follow from this method of measuring, that it is advantageous to the owner to give great breadth in proportion to length.

These two methods of admeasurement being entirely defective, I give here the view which ought to be taken of this operation, from which will be seen the method of measuring a ship exactly, in order to determine the weight it can carry.

It is known that the weight a ship can carry, is always equal to the displacement of water which that weight occasions; the question then is only to measure the part of the ship, which is to be immersed in the water by the weight of the cargo. This measurement may be made with greater or less exactness. I shall give here the process necessary to attain the object in view, which is the most simple, but at the same time the least exact.

The ship, when its admeasurement is taken, is supposed to be light; its draught of water is taken in this state forward and aft; afterwards the draught of water is determined forward and aft, which it is to have when the lading is in: hence the number of feet is known, to which each extremity must be brought down; these are added together, and half their sum taken. There are known; first, the quantity which the ship would be brought down by the effect of the lading; secondly, its length, which is measured from the wing transom; thirdly, its breadth which is taken to the outside of the plank: these three dimensions are multiplied together, and the product is divided, if the ship be full at its extremities, by 110; if on the contrary it be lean, by 115; and the quotient is the burthen of the ship in lasts. But if the vessel be a store-ship or have the form of one, keeping its greatest breadth almost the whole length, and also full at the extremities, 105 is taken for the divisor.

For example, a ship has length in a straight line before the wing transom 134 feet, and breadth to the outside of the plank 34 feet.

Suppose that it has a draught of water, when light, abaft 12 feet, forward 8 feet 7 inches; suppose also that the draught of water, when laden is abaft 19 feet, and forward 18; subtracting twelve feet from 19, 7 will remain; and subtracting 8 feet 7 inches from 18 feet, 9 feet 5 inches will remain, which added to 7 feet, will make 16 feet 5 inches, half of which is 8 feet 2 1/2 inches, which the lading should bring the ship down. Multiplying 134 feet, 34 feet, and 8 feet 2 1/2 inches together, the product will be 37400.

If the ship be a bark, or supposing it to be full in its extremities, this number must be divided by 110, and the burthen of the ship will be 340 lasts; if it be a frigate, or a ship very sharp fore and aft, the divisor will be 115, and the ship will carry 325 1/5 lasts; if this ship be fuller above and below, as well as at the extremities 112 might be used as the divisor, and it would carry 333 13/14 lasts.

This method also depends partly on the correctness of the eye, in estimating the degree, more or less, of the rising of the ship, and choosing in consequence the divisor; it is to be attained by a little attention and practice. The measurer will not be deceived thus 5 lasts; and according to the common method of measuring, he may make an error of 40 lasts for ships of this size.

One might perform the operation with more exactness, by taking more breadths independently of the middle one, and then there ought not to be an error of one last; but as this would require more time, to take the measures and make the calculations, I shall not enter upon it.

In loading a ship, it is necessary to take care to put no more on board than the lading which is consistent with its sailing.

For example: If the ship has ballast in, when measured, it is necessary to add its weight to the burden, which has been found for the vessel: but if the water, the provisions, the guns and ammunition, &c. are not on board, if there be wanting only a cable, a sail, or any thing of this kind, their weight when known must be subtracted from the burden given by the measurer.

To estimate these things, it may be supposed that provisions with the casks and wood for one man, for one month, weighs 186 provision pounds. The water also for one man for the same time 217 pounds: the man himself with his effects 260 pounds.

When the number of the ship's crew is known, the time for which it is to be provisioned and watered, it is not difficult to find the total weight of these things.

The weight of a 12 pounder with its carriage, breeching and tackle, is very nearly 13 skiponds; that of an 8 pounder with the same, is 10 skiponds; of 6, 8 skiponds; of 4, 6 skiponds; of 3, 4 1/2 skiponds; of 2, 3 1/2 skiponds; all iron weight. The powder, shot, wads, &c. should be an eighth of the weight of the gun and its carriage, in time of war; in time of peace, less.

The galley and cooking utensils (if these be not on board) may be estimated at 30lbs. for each man of the crew.

It is necessary to see in like manner if it want cables, hawsers, or other parts of the rigging. The square of the circumference of the cordage divided by 4, gives the weight of a fathom of the said cordage.

Thus it is required to find the weight of a 15 inch cable; the square of 15 is 225; dividing 225 by 4, you will have 56 1/4 lbs. for the weight of a fathom of this cable. A hundred fathoms of it will, therefore, weigh 2625 lbs. which makes nearly 14 skiponds, provision weight, or 17 skiponds, 10 lisponds, iron weight.

If the rigging be wanting altogether, it may be supposed that the weight of the whole for a ship, frigate-built, with the masts, is equal to its burden in lasts, divided by 1,88; but for a bark, which has less rigging in proportion to the lading it can carry, the divisor will be 1,98. For ketches, galeasses, howker-sloops, the divisor should be 2,5; this is sufficiently exact for the object in view.

On the accommodations for provisions

When it is necessary to make accommodations for the provisions, as bread, peas, grain, &c., supposing the number of the crew, and the time for which the ship is to be provisioned, to be known, it is easy to determine the capacity which the store-rooms should have; and it is the more necessary to make an exact calculation in this respect, because there is always in ships very little space for things which are essential, particularly in ships of war. If too much be taken for one thing, there will be space wanting for another.

For example, if we wish to know the size it is necessary to give to the bread-room of a ship with a crew of 24 men, to be provisioned for six months:

The amount of bread for one month, weighs 21 1/2 pounds; that for six months 129 pounds, and consequently 3096 pounds for the whole crew for six months. The cubic foot of biscuit weighs 26 pounds; divide this number 3096 by 26, the quotient will be 119 cubic feet, which is the space which the biscuit should take up, being well stowed.

Thus may be found the room proper for putting the peas: one man being allowed 45 quarts *per* month, that is, 270 quarts for 6 months, and consequently 6480 quarts for the whole crew, for the same time, which makes 810 kans, or 14 1/2 tons; and as the ton contains 5,6 cubic feet, multiply this quantity 5,6 by 14 1/2, the product will be 81; wherefore there will be wanted for the peas a space of 81 cubic feet.

It is necessary, however, to give a little more space than the result of the calculation, which depends on the place where the passages into the store-rooms can be worked.

In a similar manner, if the ship take three months or 91 days' water, 1 1/3 kan to a man *per* day, which will make for one man for three months 121 1/3 kans, and consequently 2912 kans for the whole crew. The space which the proper casks will take up, is found by means of their dimensions.

Thus also by the dimensions of barrels of powder, the length and diameter of cartridges filled up, the size is found which must be given to the powder room and ammunition chest, and also their distribution.